Financial Literacy: Planning for the Future

Saving for your Child's Education

Financial Literacy: Planning for the Future

Saving for your Child's Education

2020/21 Edition

GREY HOUSE PUBLISHING

FINANCIAL RATINGS SERIES

WeissRatings
& **Grey House** Publishing

https://greyhouse.weissratings.com

Grey House Publishing
4919 Route 22, PO Box 56
Amenia, NY 12501-0056
(800) 562-2139

Weiss Ratings
4400 Northcorp Parkway
Palm Beach Gardens, FL 33410
(561) 627-3300

WeissRatings
Independent. Unbiased. Accurate. Trusted.

Published by Grey House Publishing, Inc., located at 4919 Route 22, Amenia, NY 12501; telephone 518-789-8700. Grey House Publishing neither guarantees the accuracy of the data contained herein nor assumes any responsibility for errors, omissions or discrepancies. Grey House Publishing accepts no payment for listing; inclusion in the publication of any organization, agency, institution, publication, service or individual does not imply endorsement of the publisher.

Grey House Publishing

2020/21 Edition
ISBN: 978-1-64265-586-5

Table of Contents

Welcome!

Grey House Publishing and Weiss Ratings are proud to announce the third edition of *Financial Literacy: Planning for the Future*. Each volume in this series provides readers with easy-to-understand guidance on how to manage their finances. This eight-volume set assists readers who are ready for one—or more—of many important next steps in their financial planning–starting a family, buying a home, weighing insurance options, protecting themselves from identify theft, planning for college and so much more. *Financial Literacy: Planning for the Future* takes readers further towards their financial goals.

Written in easy-to-understand language, these guides take the guesswork out of financial planning. Each guide is devoted to a specific topic relevant to making big decisions with significant financial impact. Combined, these eight guides provide readers with helpful information on how to best manage their money and plan for their future and their family's future. Readers will find helpful guidance on:

- Financial Planning for **Living Together, Getting Married & Starting a Family**
- **Buying a Home**
- **Insurance Strategies** & **Estate Planning** to Protect Your Family
- Making the Right **Healthcare Coverage** Choices
- Protect Yourself from **Identify Theft & Other Scams**
- **Starting a Career** & **Career Advancement**
- **Saving for Your Child's Education**
- **Retirement Planning Strategies** & the Importance of Starting Early

Filled with valuable information alongside helpful worksheets and planners, these volumes are designed to point you in the right direction toward a solid financial future, and give you helpful guidance along the way.

Planning for the Future:
Saving for your Child's Education
Part 1: Types of Savings Plans

Saving for Your Child's Education

When your goal is to save money for your child's education, you should start as soon as possible – ideally, when your child is born. The sooner you begin with a robust savings plan, the more money you will save over time. Setting good financial goals and getting an early start are the best and most efficient ways to save for your child's college education.

While the benefits of saving early are many, saving anytime is better than not saving at all, so don't be discouraged if your child is well past infancy when you start saving for his or her education..

This guide is divided into three parts to help you get started.

1. Types of Savings Plans
2. How Much Should I Save?
3. Budgeting Strategies

Types of Savings Plans

Common ways to set aside money for a child or a grandchild include:

- **529 Education Savings Plans.** 529 Savings Plans have tax advantages and potentially other incentives to make it easier to save for college. These plans exist specifically for education savings, unlike trusts and UGMA/UTMA custodial accounts. The rest of this chapter will look at features of 529 plans that make them worth considering if you're starting to save for your child's education.

- **UGMA and UTMA Accounts.** UGMA stands for Uniform Gift to Minors Act, and UTMA stands for Uniform Transfer to Minors Act. These are custodial accounts: the account is opened in the name of the child or beneficiary, and the parent or guardian has custody over the account until the child comes of age, usually when they turn either eighteen or twenty-one. At that point, control over the account switches entirely to the beneficiary. UGMA and UTMA accounts are taxed, unlike 529 savings plans.

- *Trusts.* The benefits of opening a trust include, above all, the flexibility you will have in defining the terms of the arrangement, including conditions for the distribution of the assets. By contrast, something like a 529 education savings plan requires that the assets be used only towards the cost of college and under the rules established by the IRS. One big downside to trusts for many families is that attorneys need to be involved in order to set up and administer them; this isn't always cost-effective or convenient.

- *Educational Savings Accounts.* This is another type of tax-advantaged investment account in the United States designed to encourage savings to cover future education.

- *Savings Bonds.* Savings bonds are virtually risk-free and offer

tax benefits for higher education if owners meet certain requirements. However, their rate of return is lower than other available education savings plans.

Having a college degree is more important than ever. According to the Bureau of Labor Statistics, a person with a bachelor's degree can expect to earn an annual salary that's 64% larger than someone with only a high school diploma. **Over the course of a career, that amounts to 1.2 million additional dollars.** Of course, everyone knows that college is also more expensive than ever before, and this is why your savings plan is so important.

New to Saving?

Start Small. Decide, for example, to put just one percent of your earnings aside for the month. You can begin today. Even though you are not making a big commitment, you have crossed a threshold: you are actively involved in saving money. Going forward, it is much easier to revise your saving plan than it is to form a new one!

If you invested $10 a week into a 529 plan starting when you child is born, you would have $16,280 after 18 years. If you invested $20 a week, you would have $32,561 to help your child pay for college.

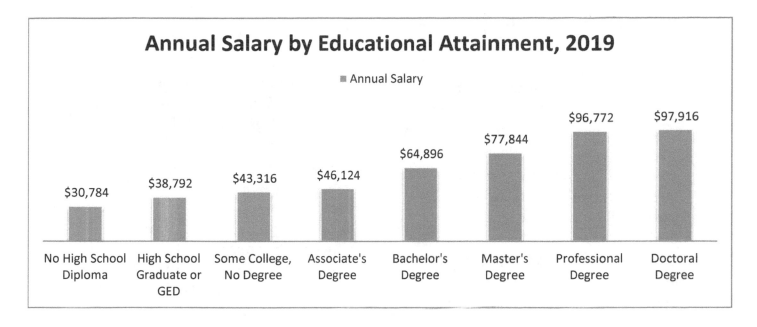

Annual Salary by Educational Attainment, 2019

■ Annual Salary

						$96,772	$97,916
					$77,844		
				$64,896			
$30,784	$38,792	$43,316	$46,124				

| No High School Diploma | High School Graduate or GED | Some College, No Degree | Associate's Degree | Bachelor's Degree | Master's Degree | Professional Degree | Doctoral Degree |

Source: https://www.bls.gov/emp/chart-unemployment-earnings-education.htm

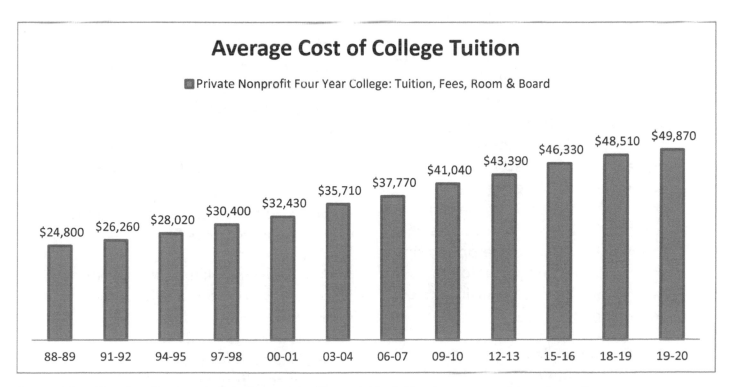

Average Cost of College Tuition

■ Private Nonprofit Four Year College: Tuition, Fees, Room & Board

| $24,800 | $26,260 | $28,020 | $30,400 | $32,430 | $35,710 | $37,770 | $41,040 | $43,390 | $46,330 | $48,510 | $49,870 |
| 88-89 | 91-92 | 94-95 | 97-98 | 00-01 | 03-04 | 06-07 | 09-10 | 12-13 | 15-16 | 18-19 | 19-20 |

Source: https://trends.collegeboard.org/college-pricing/figures-tables/tuition-fees-room-and-board-over-time

What is a 529 Plan?

According to the Internal Revenue Service, a 529 plan is a savings plan operated "by a state or educational institution, with tax advantages and potentially other incentives to make it easier to save for college and other post-secondary training, or for tuition in connection with enrollment or attendance at an elementary or secondary public, private, or religious school for a designated beneficiary, such as a child or grandchild."[1]

A 529 can be either a prepaid plan or a savings plan. A **prepaid plan** allows you to pay your child's tuition today at today's tuition rates. The credit hours purchased will be held in reserve for your child. The funds you save can be used to pay tuition at any of your state's eligible colleges or universities, or, can be transferred to a private college or a public college out of state. When you look at the increasing costs of college tuition over the years, this may be an attractive option since you're paying today's tuition rates instead of what the rate will be many years from now.

A 529 **savings plan** is much like a savings account or a 401(k)

1 www.irs.gov/newsroom/529-plans-questions-and-answers

Why 529?

An act of Congress created the 529 plan in 1997. The name comes from the number of the IRS code that deals with "Qualified Tuition Programs." That number just happened to be 529.

investment account. It differs from a regular savings account in the ways it is *tax-advantaged.* The plan's earnings are exempt from federal income taxes. They are generally exempt from state income taxes, too, so long as the plan is administered by the state of your residence. Of course, contributions made to the plan, and thus to the plan's beneficiary, are exempt from gift taxes.

The *account holder* is the person who opens the 529 plan, i.e., parent or grandparent. Your child, or the person planning to use or benefit from the money, is the *beneficiary.*

A 529 savings plan is different from other savings accounts because it is especially designed with educational goals in mind. A 529 plan helps families save for future college expenses. Beginning in 2017, the plans may also be used to pay for expenses incurred by kindergarten and elementary education – a big change from before.

529 plans are administered by the states rather than by the federal government. At the present time, 529 plans are offered by the District of Columbia and all states in the union except Wyoming. But if you're a Wyomingite, don't worry: there are a number of other state 529 plans that are available to you, and to anyone else in the country. In other words, you aren't necessarily restricted to your own state's 529, although the tax burden may be higher if you choose an out-of-state 529.

There is also a non-profit consortium of private colleges that operates a separate 529 plan. This plan is called, conveniently enough, the **private college 529 plan**. For more about the private college 529 plan, visit www.privatecollege529.com.

Benefits of a 529 Plan

529 plans give your family **income tax breaks**. You will not be taxed on the plan's earnings, and you will not be taxed when you withdraw funds from the plan as long as the funds are used for education.

- So far, 34 states offer additional **state tax incentives** with their 529 plans.

- You may be able to claim tax benefits whenever you contribute.

- You can withdraw funds from your 529 plan whenever you want, but be aware that some taxes and penalties may apply, especially if the funds are not used to pay tuition or educational expenses.

- 529 plans are easy to manage and may allow for automatic investments to make saving money easier and more reflexive.

- In some states, the money you contribute to your 529 plan does not have to be reported on your state tax return.

- 529 plans have **no income limits, age limits, or annual contribution limits**. In a real sense, the design of the 529 plan levels the playing field, making it easier for lower- and middle-income families to save for college.

- Some employers have matching contribution programs, and some states have 529 grant programs, too.

History of 529 Plans

The rising cost of college began to significantly outpace the rate of inflation over fifty years ago, creating financial burdens on families struggling to pay ever-higher tuition costs. In 1997, Section 529 of the Internal Revenue Code was amended by the Taxpayer Relief Act. The act was crafted to provide tax incentives in order to help pay for higher education. These incentives included innovations like the 529 savings plan and others that are now familiar to everyone, like deductions on student loan interest.

In 2001, there was another major overhaul to section 529. The Economic Growth and Tax Relief Reconciliation Act (EGTRRA) was passed, making the earnings in 529 plans completely **tax-free.**

The EGTRRA originally had an expiration date of December 31, 2010. This was altered by the Pension Protection Act of 2006. Since then, the tax exempt status of 529 plans is a permanent feature of the plans. Today, the tax benefit is the chief selling point.

Finally, in 2017, with the passage of the Tax Cuts and Jobs Act, the rules governing 529 plans were expanded to include K-12 tuition at private and religious schools. These plans can now be used to fund K-12 tuition costs up to $10,000 per year. That cap is likely to expand regularly.

According the Federal Reserve, as of 2019, the total assets in 529 plans were worth over $371 billion.[2]

Two Types of 529 Plans

There are two kinds of 529 plans:

- *529 Prepaid Tuition Plans*

- *529 Education Savings Plans*

529 Prepaid Tuition Plans

Prepaid plans are easy to figure out from their name—expenses are paid before the child goes to school. The private college 529 plan is a prepaid plan. It's not like a savings plans in that it does not invest your money so that you can withdraw it later to pay for your future expenses. Instead, the idea is that you can pay *now* for services consumed in the future. In other words, you are buying tomorrow's tuition at today's prices.

[2] 529 Total Plans by State. Federal Reserve Bank. https://www.federalreserve.gov/releases/efa/t otal-529-assets.pdf

The advantage to prepaid plans is that they guarantee the cost of tuition. If you have a prepaid tuition plan, you do not have to worry about the ups and downs of investing or what college costs will be in the future. You pay today and your child goes to college when he or she is ready.

Most prepaid plans use *tuition certificates*. Tuition certificates represent the tuition payments you make for each year of higher education. Participating colleges and universities are required to honor tuition certificates for up to thirty years from the date of the certificate's purchase. Some prepaid plans charge application and/or administrative fees.

It is important to research and understand the individual plans available, so that you can make an informed decision. Prepaid plans are not guaranteed or insured by the federal government. Some states guarantee their plans while others do not. Again, it is important to know the details of any plans before you invest or spend your money. Most states have information online detailing their state's plans, and most financial advisors are happy to speak with you.

529 Education Savings Plans

The second type of plan is the *education savings plan.* An education savings plan lets the account holder or saver invest money for the beneficiary's education. Just like any investment, an education savings plan may have a myriad of investment options from mutual funds to any number of bank products. There are lots of choices and investment options when exploring an education savings plan. Be sure to understand the differences and try to find the plan that works best for you and your family.

Most states have detailed information about their 529 plans available online, and there are online resources for comparing plans nationwide. A good financial advisor will tell you that tax advantages shouldn't be the only factors you examine when deciding on an education savings plan.

- Does the plan have fees?

- How has the plan performed during the last five years?

- How has it performed during the last ten years?

Remember, if you get started early, saving for college is a long-term investment.

Some Features of 529 Plans

You can find out the specifics about 529 plan options available to you in your state – and other ways to save for your child's education – by looking at your state's resources online. Every state in the union has a website devoted to 529 plans and college savings.

Typically, there are no minimum contributions required of you. This can be a big help if you want to maintain flexibility about when and how much you contribute to the account. It's a big help in making college savings attractive to lower-income people, a major goal of section 529 policy. Further, there are typically no restrictions on who may contribute to the plan. This is also a great benefit when grandparents and others decide to chip in.

There are, as you might expect, rules about the *maximum* account balance in a 529 and about how much money can be contributed per year. This is, obviously, to keep you from abusing the plan and taking advantage of its benefits by squirreling away more

About Gift Taxes and 529 Plans

- "With 5-year gift tax averaging, also known as superfunding, each contributor to a 529 college savings plan can make a lump sum contribution of up to five times the annual gift tax exclusion. A couple can jointly give double this amount. The contributions are treated as though they were spread evenly over a five-year period starting with the current calendar year. The lump sum contribution will use all or part of the annual gift tax exclusion for the beneficiary during the five-year period."

- "For example, a grandparent can give up to $75,000 in 2020 as a lump sum to each grandchild without having to pay gift taxes, based on the $15,000 annual gift tax exclusion. The grandmother and grandfather can together jointly give up to $150,000 to each grandchild. The grandparents will be unable to give any more money to each grandchild in 2020, 2021, 2022, 2023 and 2024."

Source: https://www.savingforcollege.com/article/6-year-gift-tax-averaging

money than you would use for education.

In New York, for example, as of 2020, the sum of accounts for any single beneficiary cannot exceed $520,000. The number is based on an estimate of five years of qualified education costs. Most states typically revise the number annually.

Federal tax rules now allow a single person to make a gift of up to $15,000 a year before the gift tax kicks in. That number is $30,000 for married couples. This is great if you want to set aside money for your child's future, and it's even better if you have a 529 plan. This is because there is a special provision in the law regarding 529 plans that allows a single person or married couple to contribute *five times those limits* before the money becomes taxable. This means that you can contribute $75,000 (and $150,000 if you are a married couple) in a single year to a

529 account. That's a large tax relief. The caveat is that you can't do it every year; the idea here is that you are allowed to make five-years' worth of contributions in one single year.

An increasingly important feature of 529 plans, and a cause for their rise to the top of the heap among education savings plans, is the growing trend of employer matching contribution programs. More and more companies are offering matching contributions to 529 plans, much as they already do to 401(k) plans. Unlike your 401(k) match, your will have to pay income tax on the amount received from your employer; it still counts as income.

Although the laws regarding 529 plans are established by the IRS, there is some leeway in their administration from state to state. Further, state 529 websites are usually administered in conjunction with financial firms, and you will see a wide variety of products offered and a variety of interfaces

Did you know?

- The average cost of college for an American family in the 2019/20 school year was $30,017.

- Of that figure, 44% was paid for by income and savings, 25% by scholarships and grants, and 21% was borrowed.

Source: How America Pays for College 2020. Sallie Mae Bank.
https://www.salliemae.com/about/leading-research/how-america-pays-for-college/

from state to state. Sometimes, these consumer websites will break down information on college savings options for specific categories of contributor, like *parents, grandparents* and *employer.* Others will add helpful tools regarding your investment strategies. Future Scholar, the 529 website for South Carolina (to take just one example) lists over fifteen different investment funds, and they are ranked from *aggressive* to *moderate* to *moderately conservative.*

Because 529 plans are so easy to open and because they can vary, it's especially important that you spend the time needed to find out all that you can. You might want to consult a financial adviser.

Making a large, lump sum contribution to an account like a 529 plan is often called *frontloading.* By dropping money into a savings plan early, there is more opportunity for potential growth. If, for example, you just received a windfall like a big bonus or an inheritance, you should definitely consider frontloading your child's 529 plan.

Whether you have the bounty to *frontload* a plan or you are starting with a small and humble contribution, you are making a wise decision when you open a 529 plan. Do your homework and research your state's plan. You can also compare plans between states. Every state has information available online detailing its 529 plan. Remember too that many

Your Family Can Contribute Too

If your playroom is already overcrowded, let your family know that a contribution to your child's college fund would be appreciated instead of traditional gifts for birthdays or holidays. It can be awkward to ask for money instead of gifts, so you might want to save those requests for immediate family, like grandparents, aunts, uncles and godparents.

Some 529 plans allow direct contributions from family members, either by a personalized link, a special code, or by check.

On average, children receive $200 per year in monetary gifts. If you invested these gifts every year into your child's 529 plan, you would have an extra $6,200 towards their college fund.

states, like South Carolina, have an open enrollment policy for their funds, placing very few if any restrictions on opening an account.

If you want to take a look at your state's plan or compare the state plans available across the country, you can check out one of the many websites that lets you investigate all of your 529 plan options. While you are researching, however, be aware of the fact that many financial advisors want to sell you on the plan they are representing. Make sure that the site you are using is not promoting any particular plan unless viewing the promotional details of that plan is your intention. Research well. The more you understand, the more likely you will be to make an informed decision that will pay off in the future. A 529 plan is an investment, but it is also the way to give a child a brighter future.

Where Else Can I Find Up-to-date Information about 529 Plans?

The College Savings Plans Network (CSPN), which is an arm of the National Association of State Treasurers (NAST), should be your go-to source for up-to-date and reliable information about 529 plans in general as well as specifics about plans from state to state. CSPN is a semi-official clearinghouse for information about 529 plans, and it also engages in legislative advocacy. In addition to helpful articles, CSPN has a web tool called "Plan Comparison by State" available at http://plans.collegesavings.org/planComparisonState.aspx.   We have also included a copy of CSPN's Plan Comparison by State in the Appendix of this volume.

Perhaps because so many grandparents are investing in their grandchildren's educations, the American Association of Retired Persons (AARP) has a section on their website with tools to help you understand 529 plans. You can find their information at www.aarpcollegesavings.com/tools-and-resources/tool-compare.shtml

Utilization of 529 Plans and the Future

The utilization of 529 plans has grown tremendously over the last couple of decades. In fact, Sallie Mae[3] reports that 37% of families used a college savings account like a 529 plan to pay for college in the 2019/20 academic year, compared to 21% in 2018/19. That same report says that 91% of families agree that higher education is an investment in the student's future and 82% of families believe the student will earn more money with a college degree.

Here's the big question: If the experts agree that 529 plans are one of the best ways to save for college, and statistics tell us that opening a 529 plan is a great first step in planning for success, why do so few families take advantage of saving for college with a 529 plan?

There are several factors that may affect a family's decision to save with a 529 plan.

- Families often don't save for college because they may not have the resources to save or they underestimate college costs.

- For families who do save, many don't know how a 529 plan could help them.

- Even families who want to take advantage of a 529 plan can have trouble selecting and using one.

Some of this confusion results from the fact that details regarding 529 plans vary from state to state. In 2012, for example, the GAO reported that fees associated with 529 plans could vary from 0 to 2.78 percent depending on the type of plan and the state in which it was held.

Top Tips for 529 Hunting

- **Compare plans**. Do your research. Take the time to review the plan available in your state and in other states. Each state offers a plan, and they all provide online information. It may take a little work, but investing your time will pay off.

---

[3] https://www.salliemae.com/about/leading-research/how-america-pays-for-college/

- **Know the tax advantages**. State plans differ widely, and some states do not offer any tax breaks to their residents who save. Find out what your state offers, and you will know what to look for when you compare your state's plan with others.

- **Watch for fees**. Some states may charge an enrollment fee for opening a plan. However, there may also be management fees charged for your plan. Ask questions before you invest.

 **Beyond a 529 Plan: Other College Savings Ideas**

Coverdell Education Savings Accounts

Coverdell Education Savings Accounts or ESAs are another tax-advantaged education savings plan that can be used as an alternative to – or in conjunction with – a 529 plan. Until 2017, one of the key differences between a Coverdell ESA and a 529 plan was that only the Coverdell ESA could be used for tuition below the college level. That changed in 2017, when the 529 code was expanded to include K-12 tuition costs. Many parents are rolling their Coverdell ESAs into a 529.

At present, the chief difference between a Coverdell ESA and a 529 plan is the cap. Contributions to a Coverdell ESA are currently capped at $2,000 annually – quite a bit below the current cap for 529s.

Like the 529, these accounts can only be used for education expenses. Also, when you open the account, you need to declare at the time that you are opening a Coverdell ESA – it isn't possible to open a savings account today and call it a Coverdell account tomorrow.

The tax benefits are similar to 529 plans. The money can grow without being taxed annually, and it can be withdrawn in the future tax-free in order to pay for qualified education expenses.

There are certain restrictions and requirements involved in opening a Coverdell ESA.

- The beneficiary must be either a special needs student or under the age of 18 at the time that the account is opened.

- You must specify that you are opening a Coverdell account. You can't open a savings account today and call it a Coverdell account tomorrow.

You would need to close the first account with whatever tax liability accrued on its earnings and then open a new account as a Coverdell ESA.

The big drawback of Coverdell Education Saving Accounts is that they are limited in terms of the amount you can invest. It doesn't matter if you have one Coverdell ESA or six accounts for your child—you can still only save $2,000 for the entire year.

For example, if you have two Coverdell savings accounts for the same student, you could only invest $1,000 in each for a total of $2,000. That's too small to be a realistic stand-alone college education fund, but it can help.

Moreover, contributions to the account are not tax deductible. They differ in this regard from 529 plans, in which contributions are tax deductible up to certain limits. Like the 529, contributions can only be made in cash.

The funds in a Coverdell ESA must be used by the time the student or beneficiary is thirty years of age.

Using Savings Bonds for Education

Savings bonds are a low-risk investment strategy. They are also more modest in their returns than 529 plans are, generally speaking. One of the virtues of 529 plans is the variety of investment risk options available to you. Nevertheless, savings bonds are very safe; they are backed fully by the U.S. government. Both the principal and the earned interest are guaranteed and are not subject to market fluctuations. And, because, savings bonds are registered with the Treasury Department, they can always be replaced at no cost if they are lost or stolen. Still, you should always keep them in a safe place!

The Federal government has an **Education Bond Program** for those interested in using bonds to save for their children's education. This program makes the interest earned on some kinds of savings bonds *tax-free* when those bonds are redeemed to pay for higher education.

The bonds that are eligible include all Series EE Bonds issued after December 31, 1989, and all Series I Bonds. Series HH bonds, by contrast, are not eligible.

If you are interested in saving for your child's education using savings bonds, you should research carefully and understand the bond's requirements. For example, you might only be able to redeem the bonds in the same tax year that the beneficiary will use them.

Because of age restrictions, the student or child who will benefit from the bond cannot generally be listed as a co-owner of the bond. Only parents and/or a guardian may be acknowledged as the owners or co-owners.

Also, if you are using bonds to pay for your own educational expenses, you must be the person listed as the owner of the bonds.

Additional Funding Sources for College

For many families, parents' income and savings is not the only source of funding to pay for their child's college education. Scholarships, grants, student loans and other sources can help pay for the full cost of college.

Sallie Mae's 2020 report[4] shows that parents' income and savings make up 44% of college costs, but the other 56% is made up of student income and savings, student borrowing, scholarships and grants, relatives, and parent borrowing.

Take a look at the chart on the next page for a breakdown of the average sources of college funding.

Knowing this can also help you prepare your savings goals. As a parent, you might want to have a goal to pay for half of your child's education, with the remaining half made up of scholarships, grants, student savings, and student loans. You'll find more information in the next section that will help you answer the question, "How much should I save?"

---

[4] https://www.salliemae.com/about/leading-research/how-america-pays-for-college/

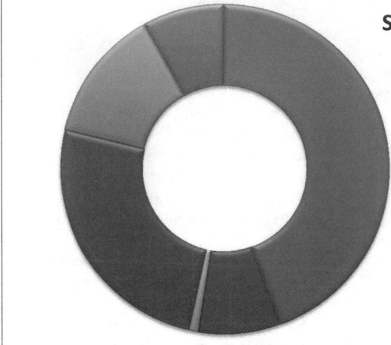

Sources of College Funding

- Parent income & savings (44%)
- Parent borrowing (8%)

- Relatives (1%)

- Scholarships & grants (25%)

- Student borrowing (13%)

- Student income & savings (8%)

Get Started!

Whether you choose a 529 plan, choose to buy savings bonds as a low-risk investment strategy, or choose to open a simple savings account and pay into it regularly, you will find that saving money for college works best if you are disciplined enough to make saving a part of your monthly routine. Prepare and find as many ways to save as you can. The best time to get started saving for your child's college is now.

Part 2: How Much Should I Save?

How Much Should I Save?

How much you plan to save for your child's education will vary on a number of factors.

- **Do you want to cover all of your child's college expenses?**

  Many parents don't plan on paying for 100% of their child's education. Instead, they might plan to pay for half of their child's tuition, and the balance will be paid for by a combination of grants, scholarships, work-study programs and student loans.

- **Do you want to plan to pay for tuition for an in-state college or a private college?**

  On average, the average tuition at a public four-year college is $10,440 per year, compared to a private four-year college at $36,880 per year.

- **Do you want to pay for two or four years of college?**

  Some parents plan on paying a portion of their child's tuition for four years. Others might plan on paying for the first two years of college.

Type of College	Average Annual Tuition & Fees: 2019/20 Academic Year
Public Two-Year College (in-district students)	$3,730
Public Four-Year College (in-state students)	$10,440
Public Four-Year College (out-of-state students)	$26,820
Private Four-Year College	$36,880

Source: Trends in College Pricing, https://trends.collegeboard.org/college-pricing

- **How much time do you have?**

  Starting early is very important, if you want to take the most advantage of your savings plan. When you factor in compound interest, the earlier you start saving, the more opportunity you have to earn interest on what you have already saved.

- **How many children do you have?**

  The more children you have to save for, the more important it is to start early.

- **How much can you afford?**

  If you start early, make a budget, and stay on track, you'll be well on your way to saving for your child's education. Even if you're only able to save $20 a week, that savings will add up over time.

  You might be surprised at how quickly your savings will add up; see the following charts.

Sample Savings Plan 1

Parent plans to pay for 50% of the tuition and fees at a public two-year college (in-district) for one child.

Type of School: .... Public College, In-District

Parent Contribution ....50% of tuition

Years of College.. 2

Savings Goal: $7,351

Start Saving at Age	Annual Savings Contribution	Savings Contribution per Week
0	$ 224.70	$ 4.32
2	$ 245.88	$ 4.72
4	$ 272.20	$ 5.23
6	$ 305.86	$ 5.88
8	$ 350.55	$ 6.74
10	$ 412.88	$ 7.94
12	$ 506.13	$ 9.73

Estimated figures were calculated using the College Savings Calculator provided by FINRA at https://tools.finra.org/college_savings/ using an annual return of 5.25%. The rising cost of tuition is calculated at 3.8% per year, which means that a $3,730 annual tuition in 2020 would be $7,298 per year in 2038.

Important: The FINRA calculator was designed to help investors evaluate basic college savings scenarios. Please understand its limitations and note that the results are hypothetical. This tool does not take into consideration any potential tax impacts. Some savings products may include additional fees not factored into this tool's results. As a result, your results will be higher or lower than those shown.

Sample Savings Plan 2

Parent plans to pay for 75% of the tuition and fees at a public two-year college (in-district) for one child.

Type of School: .... Public College, In-District

Parent Contribution ....75% of tuition

Years of College.. 2

Savings Goal: $11,027

Start Saving at Age	Annual Savings Contribution	Savings Contribution per Week
0	$ 337.05	$ 6.48
2	$ 368.83	$ 7.09
4	$ 408.30	$ 7.85
6	$ 458.79	$ 8.82
8	$ 525.82	$ 10.11
10	$ 619.33	$ 11.91
12	$ 759.20	$ 14.60

Estimated figures were calculated using the College Savings Calculator provided by FINRA at https://tools.finra.org/college_savings/ using an annual return of 5.25%. The rising cost of tuition is calculated at 3.8% per year, which means that a $3,730 annual tuition in 2020 would be $7,298 per year in 2038.

Important: The FINRA calculator was designed to help investors evaluate basic college savings scenarios. Please understand its limitations and note that the results are hypothetical. This tool does not take into consideration any potential tax impacts. Some savings products may include additional fees not factored into this tool's results. As a result, your results will be higher or lower than those shown.

Sample Savings Plan 3

Parent plans to pay for 100% of the tuition and fees at a public two-year college (in-district) for one child.

Type of School: .... Public College, In-District

Parent Contribution .... 100% of tuition

Years of College 2

Savings Goal: $14,703

Start Saving at Age	Annual Savings Contribution	Savings Contribution per Week
0	$ 449.40	$ 8.64
2	$ 491.77	$ 9.45
4	$ 544.40	$ 10.46
6	$ 611.73	$ 11.76
8	$ 701.09	$ 13.48
10	$ 825.77	$ 15.88
12	$ 1,012.27	$ 19.46

Estimated figures were calculated using the College Savings Calculator provided by FINRA at https://tools.finra.org/college_savings/ using an annual return of 5.25%. The rising cost of tuition is calculated at 3.8% per year, which means that a $3,730 annual tuition in 2020 would be $7,298 per year in 2038.

Important: The FINRA calculator was designed to help investors evaluate basic college savings scenarios. Please understand its limitations and note that the results are hypothetical. This tool does not take into consideration any potential tax impacts. Some savings products may include additional fees not factored into this tool's results. As a result, your results will be higher or lower than those shown.

Sample Savings Plan 4

Parent plans to pay for 50% of the tuition and fees at a public four-year college (in-state) for one child.

Type of School: .... Public College, In-State

Parent Contribution .... 50% of tuition

Years of College 4

Savings Goal: $43,247

Start Saving at Age	Annual Savings Contribution	Savings Contribution per Week
0	$ 1,176.42	$ 22.62
2	$ 1,275.52	$ 24.52
4	$ 1,395.78	$ 26.84
6	$ 1,545.18	$ 29.71
8	$ 1,736.26	$ 33.38
10	$ 1,989.91	$ 38.26
12	$ 2,343.78	$ 45.07

Estimated figures were calculated using the College Savings Calculator provided by FINRA at https://tools.finra.org/college_savings/ using an annual return of 5.25%. The rising cost of tuition is calculated at 3.8% per year, which means that a $10,440 annual tuition in 2020 would be $20,429 per year in 2038.

Important: The FINRA calculator was designed to help investors evaluate basic college savings scenarios. Please understand its limitations and note that the results are hypothetical. This tool does not take into consideration any potential tax impacts. Some savings products may include additional fees not factored into this tool's results. As a result, your results will be higher or lower than those shown.

Sample Savings Plan 5

Parent plans to pay for 75% of the tuition and fees at a public four-year college (in-state) for one child.

Type of School: .... Public College, In-State

Parent Contribution ....75% of tuition

Years of College... 4

Savings Goal: $64,870

Start Saving at Age	Annual Savings Contribution	Savings Contribution per Week
0	$ 1,764.63	$ 33.93
2	$ 1,913.29	$ 36.79
4	$ 2,093.68	$ 40.26
6	$ 2,317.78	$ 44.57
8	$ 2,604.39	$ 50.08
10	$ 2,984.87	$ 57.40
12	$ 3,515.67	$ 67.60

Estimated figures were calculated using the College Savings Calculator provided by FINRA at https://tools.finra.org/college_savings/ using an annual return of 5.25%. The rising cost of tuition is calculated at 3.8% per year, which means that a $10,440 annual tuition in 2020 would be $20,429 per year in 2038.

Important: The FINRA calculator was designed to help investors evaluate basic college savings scenarios. Please understand its limitations and note that the results are hypothetical. This tool does not take into consideration any potential tax impacts. Some savings products may include additional fees not factored into this tool's results. As a result, your results will be higher or lower than those shown.

Sample Savings Plan 6

Parent plans to pay for 100% of the tuition and fees at a public four-year college (in-state) for one child.

Type of School: .... Public College, In-State

Parent Contribution ....100% of tuition

Years of College.. 4

Savings Goal: $86,494

Start Saving at Age	Annual Savings Contribution	Savings Contribution per Week
0	$ 2,352.85	$ 45.24
2	$ 2,551.05	$ 49.05
4	$ 2,791.57	$ 53.67
6	$ 3,090.37	$ 59.43
8	$ 3,472.52	$ 66.77
10	$ 3,979.83	$ 76.53
12	$ 4,687.56	$ 90.14

Estimated figures were calculated using the College Savings Calculator provided by FINRA at https://tools.finra.org/college_savings/ using an annual return of 5.25%. The rising cost of tuition is calculated at 3.8% per year, which means that a $10,440 annual tuition in 2020 would be $20,429 per year in 2038.

Important: The FINRA calculator was designed to help investors evaluate basic college savings scenarios. Please understand its limitations and note that the results are hypothetical. This tool does not take into consideration any potential tax impacts. Some savings products may include additional fees not factored into this tool's results. As a result, your results will be higher or lower than those shown.

Sample Savings Plan 7

Parent plans to pay for 50% of the tuition and fees at a public four-year college (out-of-state) for one child.

Type of School: ....Public College, Out-of-State

Parent Contribution ....50% of tuition

Years of College.. 4

Savings Goal: $111,100

Start Saving at Age	Annual Savings Contribution	Savings Contribution per Week
0	$ 3,022.19	$ 58.11
2	$ 3,276.78	$ 63.01
4	$ 3,585.72	$ 68.95
6	$ 3,969.52	$ 76.33
8	$ 4,460.39	$ 85.77
10	$ 5,112.02	$ 98.30
12	$ 6,021.08	$ 115.79

Estimated figures were calculated using the College Savings Calculator provided by FINRA at https://tools.finra.org/college_savings/ using an annual return of 5.25%. The rising cost of tuition is calculated at 3.8% per year, which means that a $26,820 annual tuition in 2020 would be $52,482 per year in 2038.

Important: The FINRA calculator was designed to help investors evaluate basic college savings scenarios. Please understand its limitations and note that the results are hypothetical. This tool does not take into consideration any potential tax impacts. Some savings products may include additional fees not factored into this tool's results. As a result, your results will be higher or lower than those shown.

Sample Savings Plan 8

Parent plans to pay for 75% of the tuition and fees at a public four-year college (out-of-state) for one child.

Type of School: ....Public College, Out-of-State

Parent Contribution ....75% of tuition

Years of College.. 4

Savings Goal: $166,650

Start Saving at Age	Annual Savings Contribution	Savings Contribution per Week
0	$ 4,533.28	$ 87.17
2	$ 4,915.16	$ 94.52
4	$ 5,378.59	$ 103.43
6	$ 5,954.29	$ 114.50
8	$ 6,690.58	$ 128.66
10	$ 7,668.03	$ 147.46
12	$ 9,031.63	$ 173.68

Estimated figures were calculated using the College Savings Calculator provided by FINRA at https://tools.finra.org/college_savings/ using an annual return of 5.25%. The rising cost of tuition is calculated at 3.8% per year, which means that a $26,820 annual tuition in 2020 would be $52,482 per year in 2038.

Important: The FINRA calculator was designed to help investors evaluate basic college savings scenarios. Please understand its limitations and note that the results are hypothetical. This tool does not take into consideration any potential tax impacts. Some savings products may include additional fees not factored into this tool's results. As a result, your results will be higher or lower than those shown.

Sample Savings Plan 9

Parent plans to pay for 100% of the tuition and fees at a public four-year college (out-of-state) for one child.

Type of School: ....Public College, Out-of-State

Parent Contribution ....100% of tuition

Years of College... 4

Savings Goal: $222,200

Start Saving at Age	Annual Savings Contribution	Savings Contribution per Week
0	$ 6,044.38	$ 116.23
2	$ 6,553.55	$ 126.02
4	$ 7,171.45	$ 137.91
6	$ 7,939.05	$ 152.67
8	$ 8,920.78	$ 171.55
10	$ 10,224.04	$ 196.61
12	$ 12,042.17	$ 231.58

Estimated figures were calculated using the College Savings Calculator provided by FINRA at https://tools.finra.org/college_savings/ using an annual return of 5.25%. The rising cost of tuition is calculated at 3.8% per year, which means that a $26,820 annual tuition in 2020 would be $52,482 per year in 2038.

Important: The FINRA calculator was designed to help investors evaluate basic college savings scenarios. Please understand its limitations and note that the results are hypothetical. This tool does not take into consideration any potential tax impacts. Some savings products may include additional fees not factored into this tool's results. As a result, your results will be higher or lower than those shown.

Sample Savings Plan 10

Parent plans to pay for 50% of the tuition and fees at a private four-year college for one child.

Type of School: ....Private College

Parent Contribution ....50% of tuition

Years of College.. 4

Savings Goal: $152,773

Start Saving at Age	Annual Savings Contribution	Savings Contribution per Week
0	$ 4,155.79	$ 79.91
2	$ 4,505.87	$ 86.65
4	$ 4,930.70	$ 94.82
6	$ 5,458.46	$ 104.97
8	$ 6,133.45	$ 117.95
10	$ 7,029.50	$ 135.18
12	$ 8,279.55	$ 159.22

Estimated figures were calculated using the College Savings Calculator provided by FINRA at https://tools.finra.org/college_savings/ using an annual return of 5.25%. The rising cost of tuition is calculated at 3.8% per year, which means that a $36,880 annual tuition in 2020 would be $72,167 per year in 2038.

Important: The FINRA calculator was designed to help investors evaluate basic college savings scenarios. Please understand its limitations and note that the results are hypothetical. This tool does not take into consideration any potential tax impacts. Some savings products may include additional fees not factored into this tool's results. As a result, your results will be higher or lower than those shown.

Sample Savings Plan 11

Parent plans to pay for 75% of the tuition and fees at a private four-year college for one child.

Type of School: ....Private College

Parent Contribution ....75% of tuition

Years of College.. 4

Savings Goal: $222,639

Start Saving at Age	Annual Savings Contribution	Savings Contribution per Week
0	$ 6,233.69	$ 119.87
2	$ 6,758.81	$ 129.97
4	$ 7,396.06	$ 142.23
6	$ 8,187.70	$ 157.45
8	$ 9,200.18	$ 176.92
10	$ 10,544.25	$ 202.77
12	$ 12,419.33	$ 238.83

Estimated figures were calculated using the College Savings Calculator provided by FINRA at https://tools.finra.org/college_savings/ using an annual return of 5.25%. The rising cost of tuition is calculated at 3.8% per year, which means that a $36,880 annual tuition in 2020 would be $72,167 per year in 2038.

Important: The FINRA calculator was designed to help investors evaluate basic college savings scenarios. Please understand its limitations and note that the results are hypothetical. This tool does not take into consideration any potential tax impacts. Some savings products may include additional fees not factored into this tool's results. As a result, your results will be higher or lower than those shown.

Sample Savings Plan 12

Parent plans to pay for 100% of the tuition and fees at a private four-year college for one child.

Type of School: ....Private College

Parent Contribution ....100% of tuition

Years of College.. 4

Savings Goal: $305,546

Start Saving at Age	Annual Savings Contribution	Savings Contribution per Week
0	$ 8,311.58	$ 159.83
2	$ 9,011.75	$ 173.30
4	$ 9,861.41	$ 189.64
6	$ 10,916.93	$ 209.94
8	$ 12,266.90	$ 235.90
10	$ 14,059.01	$ 270.36
12	$ 16,559.11	$ 318.44

Estimated figures were calculated using the College Savings Calculator provided by FINRA at https://tools.finra.org/college_savings/ using an annual return of 5.25%. The rising cost of tuition is calculated at 3.8% per year, which means that a $36,880 annual tuition in 2020 would be $72,167 per year in 2038.

Important: The FINRA calculator was designed to help investors evaluate basic college savings scenarios. Please understand its limitations and note that the results are hypothetical. This tool does not take into consideration any potential tax impacts. Some savings products may include additional fees not factored into this tool's results. As a result, your results will be higher or lower than those shown.

Part 3: Budgeting Strategies to Help Get Started

Spending Now & Saving for the Future

Every family has to negotiate the trade-off between spending money and saving it. You want your family to be prepared for the future, but you also want to fulfill your family's needs today. How do you strike a balance?

It's important, of course, to incorporate savings into your monthly budget. Remember that wealth isn't technically the measure of how much you earn. It's what you have accumulated from your earnings. Or, as Benjamin Franklin reminded us, *if you would be wealthy, think of saving as well as getting.*

> Make sure that saving for your child's college fund doesn't interfere with your own retirement planning. Although there are loans for college, there are no loans to fund your retirement!

Make a Budget

The first step in making a budget is to consider how much you earn. You might be paid weekly, or biweekly, or on some other schedule, but a good number to focus on is a monthly amount. If your hours vary, look at the last six to twelve months and calculate your average monthly wages. Also consider any other income you have, such as tips, commissions, or infrequent work, interest earned on investments, as well as funds you receive from other sources such as family.

Then figure out where your money goes. Track all of your family's daily expenses for a month—every box of cereal and trip to the movies. Write down what you spend each day and what it is for. Use a spreadsheet. Account for every penny. Your expenses will fall into three categories:

1. Fixed needs

2. Variable needs

3. Wants

Budget Worksheet

Month/Year: _____

Monthly Income

Wages	_____
Tips	_____
Other Income	_____
TOTAL MONTHLY INCOME	_____

Monthly Expenses

HOUSING	Mortgage/Rent	_____
	Utilities (Electricity/Water)	_____
	Credit Cards	_____
	Insurance (Homeowner's, Renters, etc.)	_____
	Loan Payments	_____
	Other Housing Expenses (Cable, Internet, etc.)	_____
FOOD	Groceries/Household Supplies	_____
	Restaurant and Other Food	_____
TRANSPORTATION	Public Transportation	_____
	Vehicle Loan	_____
	Gas for Personal Vehicle	_____
	Parking, Tolls, etc.	_____
	Maintenance & Supplies (oil, etc.)	_____
	Vehicle Insurance	_____
HEALTH	Health Insurance	_____
	Medicine/Prescriptions	_____
	Other (Dental, Vision, Copays)	_____
PERSONAL	Childcare or Support	_____
	Clothing, Shoes, Laundry, etc.	_____
	Charitable Gifts, Donations, etc.	_____
	Entertainment (Movies, etc.)	_____
	Other (Haircuts, etc.)	_____
SAVINGS	Retirement Savings	_____
	Education Savings	_____
	Other Savings	_____
DEBT & FINANCE	Debt (Credit Cards, etc.)	_____
	Student Loans or Other Debts	_____
	Fees (Bank, Credit Card, Debit)	_____
	Prepaid Cards, Phone Cards, etc.	_____
MISCELLANEOUS EXPENSES	Pet Care	_____
	Other	_____
	TOTAL MONTHLY EXPENSES	_____

TOTAL MONTHLY INCOME	_____
- TOTAL MONTHLY EXPENSES	_____
=	_____

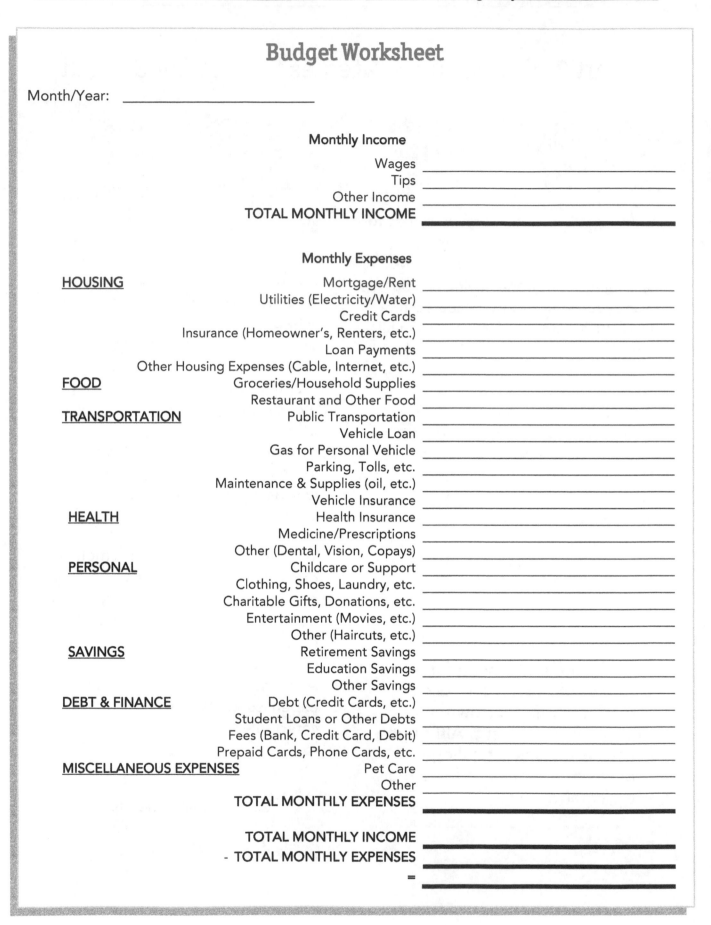

Fixed needs are necessary and usually the same from month to month. They include expenses such as housing, phone bill, car payment, student loan payment, credit card payment, and electric bill.

Variable needs are also necessities but they are not the same from month to month. They include expenses such as gas, food, pet supplies, and necessary clothing.

Wants, on the other hand, are unessential expenses. They might include meals at restaurants, movies, gym memberships, electronics, gifts, and unnecessary clothing.

Add the total amount of money you spend in a month on fixed needs, variable needs, and wants. Then subtract your monthly expenses from your monthly earnings. If you have a surplus—money left over after your expenses—you are in good shape.

However, you still may be able to cut back on unnecessary expenses and save money. If you are in the red— your expenses are greater than your earnings each month—you need to reduce expenses, increase your earnings, or both.

Other Budgeting Strategies

Some money experts believe in a simple method called the 50/30/20 rule to keep from spending more than you earn.

According to this rule, you should budget your after-tax earnings (net income) in this way:

- **Needs** should be 50 percent of your net income

- **Wants** should be 30 percent of your net income

- **Financial goals** (personal savings, savings for college, and debt reduction) should be 20 percent of your net income

These ratios are the maximum you should spend on these categories—if you can get by with less, you can save more. When following the 50/30/20 rule, you should consider where any new expense fits into these three categories. If you cannot fit it into the appropriate ratio, it does not fit into your budget. This plan is flexible, especially if you are still trying to get your finances under control. Your needs may consume more than 50 percent of your net income, for example, leaving you less to devote to financial goals. When you are in a better financial position, adjust your ratios to move closer to 50/30/20.

Keeping your "needs" at 50% of your take home pay helps you if you become injured or unemployed, since most disability payments and unemployment benefits will only be 50% of your regular salary.

Budgeting & Savings Apps

There are many tools available to help you budget your money and save money.

Budgeting Apps

These services offer real-time tools so you can see how you are spending your money each month and can alert you if you are overspending. Some of the most popular budgeting apps are:

- **Mint:** mint.com

- **PocketGuard:** pocketguard.com

- **You Need a Budget:** youneedabudget.com

- **Wally:** wally.me

- **Mvelopes:** mvelopes.com

- **GoodBudget:** goodbudget.com

- **EveryDollar:** everydollar.com

- **Clarity Money:** marcus.com

- **Buxfer:** buxfer.com

- **PearBudget:** pearbudget.com

Saving Apps

These services offer tools to help you save money. Maybe you're on a tight budget and you want to save wherever you can to create a "rainy day fund." Maybe you want to save for a large purchase like a special trip or a down-payment on a car.

Some of these apps round up your purchase to the next dollar and add the change to your savings account. If you've ever cashed in a change jar, you know how much these few cents can add up.

Be sure to review the terms carefully, since some savings apps charge a monthly fee for their service.

These savings apps can help you reach your goal:

- **Acorns:** acorns.com

- **Digit:** digit.com

- **Chime Bank:** chimebank.com

- **Trim:** asktrim.com

- **Stash:** stashinvest.com

- **Clarity Money:** claritymoney.com

- **Mint:** mint.com

- **Qapital:** qapital.com

- **Aspiration:** aspiration.com

- **Twine:** twine.com

- **Varo :** varomoney.com

- **Stash:** stashinvest.com

- **Capital One 360 Savings:** capitalone.com

- **Empower Finance:** empower.me

Ways to Save

When you look at your income and spending, you may see that you need to cut back. You might not have any money left at the end of the month to start saving for college. Look first at your list of wants. What can you eliminate?

Avoid temptation and move money into savings first

If your employer offers direct deposit, set up an automatic deposit into your education savings account. That way it isn't a temptation to spend instead. If you employer does not offer direct deposit, you can do it yourself by transferring money into your savings account when you deposit each pay check.

Check out local thrift stores and consignment stores

Children grow out of clothes, shoes and toys so quickly, if you are always buying new items, the cost will add up. You may be able to find just what you're looking for at a consignment store for a fraction of the price. You can also host a neighborhood clothing swap. Friends and family with older children are a good source for secondhand items too.

Research a nanny share

With a nanny share multiple parents split the cost of a nanny. The nanny either cares for multiple children together, or shares time between families.

Budget for holiday spending

Create a budget for holiday spending well in advance, so you don't overspend. Buying off season when prices are low is a good way to stretch your dollars.

Birthday parties don't have to break the bank

Plan a fun activity with a small group of friends. Get creative! Kids will have lot of fun with a backyard scavenger hunt or obstacle course, at the fraction of the cost of a party at an expensive venue.

How much money do you spend eating out?

Are you spending a lot on smoothies or coffee every week? What about clothes and shopping? Could you cut back on these?

If you buy a coffee every morning on the way to work, at $3 each, that works out to $780 per year. If you eat out for lunch every day, and spend $15 per day, that's $3,900 per year. If you cut back on going out for coffee and lunch, just 3 days a week, that would be an extra $2,808 in your bank account each year. Purchasing a good coffee maker and brewing it yourself will easily cut costs.

Scrutinize your spending on unnecessary items or activities

You may be able to save some of this money instead of spending it. For example, you may drop several dollars a week into vending machines for snacks during work hours. Instead, keep a supply of inexpensive snacks on hand. A box of granola bars purchased from a grocery store is

much less expensive than purchasing individual bars on the go.

Here are some tips to cut back on your grocery bills:

- Choose less-costly brands
- Look for coupons for products you buy
- Shop at a discount store
- Examine store circulars to find the best prices and buy what's on sale
- Plan your meals for the week to take advantage of sales and avoid wasting food
- Make a shopping list and stick to it, this will avoid expensive impulse purchases
- Brown bag your lunch instead of going to restaurants
- Buy in bulk
- Compare prices between different grocery stores, you may be able to save by shopping at a different store

If you usually throw away fresh fruits and vegetables because they spoil before you eat them, shop for frozen or canned produce, or buy seasonal fresh produce, which is usually less expensive.

Larger packages of food and other items are usually less costly. Check the store shelf for the unit price. The unit price tells you how much each unit, such as an ounce, of the item costs. A large box of cereal, for example, may cost more than a small box, but the cost per ounce might be much less. If small boxes are on sale, however, the unit price may be lower.

The same is true of proteins. Meats are often expensive, but they can be more affordable if you purchase large packs. Separate the meat into smaller portions—the amount you will cook for a meal—wrap it in freezer paper or bags, and freeze it. You may also consider cooking it all at once before freezing it to save time later. You could also freeze portions for two meals and have the leftovers for lunch the next day.

You can also save money by going meatless occasionally. Substituting beans, eggs, or another protein for meat once or twice a week will save on your food bill.

Try substitution instead of outright elimination

Research a less-expensive gym, or quit the gym and put the membership fees toward the purchase of home fitness equipment.

Are you paying for a streaming service to listen to music without ads? Consider using a free service instead; the interruptions are a small inconvenience if you can save money. Or, see if your local library makes

music and movie streaming services available to their library card holders.

If reducing "wants" is not enough, you may have to adjust variables

Maybe, for example, you can reduce car trips to save money on gas, or you can take public transportation more often to avoid parking fees. Share transportation expenses by carpooling with coworkers, if possible.

In some cities, you may be able to enroll in a car-sharing service, or use on-demand car services. These solutions relieve you of the expense of car payments, fuel, repairs, and car insurance.

Some areas offer alternative transportation, such as bike-sharing programs, that may also work for you. Your situation may allow you to use a variety of these transportation solutions and greatly reduce your expenses.

Learn to fix things instead of replacing them

You can find library books and online tutorials about almost any subject. Learn to sew on a button, change a tire, fix a leaky faucet, or remove a carpet stain.

Substitute handmade gifts/services for store-bought

Offer help, such as babysitting, to new parents instead of buying toys or clothes. Learn to knit or crochet and make clothing, toys, and housewares to serve as gifts. Cook or bake for friends. Organize a potluck instead of dinner at a restaurant.

Find a less-expensive housing option

The cheapest apartment is not always the best—your safety is important, as is the location where you live. If you live close to where you work or go to school, you will probably save on transportation.

Other ways to save include shopping for utilities if you are able, substituting a pay-as-you-go cell phone for a monthly contract, and shopping for less-costly insurance. You might consider cutting out cable and subscribing to a streaming service for entertainment.

Look at any fees you pay

Debit cards are convenient, but you may incur charges when using them. Your financial institution may let you make a set number of debit payments a month without adding fees, but it may charge you for using the debit card other times.

If you are racking up debit card fees, consider using a cash system—withdraw the money you can spend each pay period in one transaction. Find out if your financial institution offers any other ways to avoid fees when using your debit card. You may be able to replace the card with a debit/credit card. Making transactions as credit charges still limits you to spending only money that is in your account, but you may avoid debit fees with these purchases. Credit transactions also provide consumer protection. This means the credit company will help you in a dispute about a purchase with a merchant.

You may also pay fees for bank accounts, so it pays to shop around. Some banks offer free checking accounts to customers with direct deposit. You may be offered overdraft protection, which covers you if you try to use more money than you have in your account. The bank will allow the transaction to go through and cover your shortfall, but will charge a fee to your account in addition to the money you now owe. You can protect yourself from overdraft fees by keeping a careful watch on spending.

Ways to save on entertainment

There are many ways to save and still have fun!

Call your cable provider and explore alternate plans for a lesser fee.

Consider streaming options, like Netflix, Hulu or Sling as an alternative to cable.

Explore your cellular options. You may be able to save by switching carriers or switching plans. If you're not using very much data, you may be wasting money on an unlimited data plan. But, pay attention to fees. If you are paying overage fees for data, you're probably not in the right plan. You can also put a cap on your data plan, so if you reach your limit, you have slower access until you reach your next billing cycle.

Visit your library. Your library most likely has a wide selection of DVDs and audio books, all for free. Plus, they have books, of course. Many libraries also participate in free pass programs where you can "check out" a free or reduced cost pass to a local attraction or museum. Your local library might also offer free access to music and movie streaming.

Stay in with friends. Consider a game night and spend the night in; this can be far less expensive than a night out on the town.

Visit museums and national parks, which are free or low-cost. Go hiking or have a picnic. Be creative!

Save For Yourself Too

Don't forget about yourself. Experts recommend to fund your savings accounts in this order:

1. **Take Care of Needs.** Pay the mortgage and the grocery bills first. Don't start saving for college until your family's immediate needs are set. If you're struggling in this area, look for ways to reduce your expenses, or ways to increase your income.

2. **Save for Retirement.** This is important! Your child will be able to take out a loan for college, but there are no loans for retirement. So, make sure your retirement savings is well under way before saving for college.

3. **Save for College.** Start as early as you can, when you are financially able. Even if you contribute $20 a week into your child's college fund, you are headed in the right direction.

4. **Contribute to Your Savings.** It's important to have an emergency fund, for those unplanned expenses.

All in all, the best advice for saving for your child's education is to put a little money aside, as early as you can. The earlier you start, the more you will earn in interest, and the bigger your college fund will be.

Appendices

Helpful Resources

Contact any of the following organizations for further information about saving for your child's education.

- **U.S. Department of Education** - https://www.ed.gov/

- **Your State Department of Education** – view a complete list here: https://www2.ed.gov/about/contacts/state/index.html

- **College Savings Plan Network** - http://www.collegesavings.org

- **FINRA College Savings Calculator** - https://tools.finra.org/college_savings

529 Plans: Comparisons by State

Alabama	CollegeCounts 529 Fund	CollegeCounts 529 Fund Advisor Plan
Plan Type(s):	Direct-sold	Advisor-sold
Plan Website:	http://www.collegecounts529.com/	http://www.collegecounts529advisor.com/
Plan Residency:	NO No state residency requirements.	NO No state residency requirements.
State Tax Credit or Deduction?	YES The amount contributed by an Alabama taxpayer during a tax year is deductible from Alabama income in an amount not to exceed $5,000 for a single return or $10,000 for a joint return for that tax year. If you also contribute to another Alabama 529 account, your maximum total deduction on all contributions is still $5,000 per year ($10,000 for married couples filing jointly). Rollovers to another state's 529 plan or nonqualified withdrawals may be subject to recapture.	YES The amount contributed by an Alabama taxpayer during a tax year is deductible from Alabama income in an amount not to exceed $5,000 for a single return or $10,000 for a joint return for that tax year. If you also contribute to another Alabama 529 account, your maximum total deduction on all contributions is still $5,000 per year ($10,000 for married couples filing jointly). Rollovers to another state's 529 plan or nonqualified withdrawals may be subject to recapture.
State Tax Deferred Earnings/ Withdrawals?	YES Qualified withdrawals from the Alabama CollegeCounts 529 Fund are exempt from Alabama State income tax. Please review the Program Disclosure Statement and Account Agreement.	YES Qualified withdrawals for college are exempt from Alabama State income tax. Please review the Program Disclosure Statement and Account Agreement.
Financial Aid Benefits?	NO	NO
State Matching Grants?	NO	NO
Reward Programs?	YES Earn 1.529% on your everyday spending! Save even more for college with the CollegeCounts 529 Rewards Visa® Card. As the cost of a college education continues to rise, we've come up with a new way to help you save. With the CollegeCounts 529 Rewards Visa® Card, you can earn 1.529% on your everyday purchases. Each quarter, once you've accumulated $50 or more in rewards, the funds will be automatically invested into the CollegeCounts account(s) you designate. It's simple to earn these rewards. Just use the CollegeCounts 529 Rewards Visa® Card for your regular spending, and 1.529% of your eligible net purchases will be invested directly into your CollegeCounts account each quarter.	YES Earn 1.529% on your everyday spending! Save even more for college with the CollegeCounts 529 Rewards Visa® Card. As the cost of a college education continues to rise, we've come up with a new way to help you save. With the CollegeCounts 529 Rewards Visa® Card, you can earn 1.529% on your everyday purchases. Each quarter, once you've accumulated $50 or more in rewards, the funds will be automatically invested into the CollegeCounts account(s) you designate. It's simple to earn these rewards. Just use the CollegeCounts 529 Rewards Visa® Card for your regular spending, and 1.529% of your eligible net purchases will be invested directly into your CollegeCounts account each quarter.
Direct-sold plan fees:	0.29% - 0.89%	This is an advisor-sold plan.
Advisor-sold plan fees:	This is a direct-sold plan.	0.44% - 2.17%
Enrollment Fees:	$0	$0
Investment Option Type(s):	Age-based, Blended, Capital Preservation, Equity, Fixed Income	Age-based, Blended, Capital Preservation, Equity, Fixed Income
Min. Initial Contribution:	Minimum initial contribution: $0.00	Minimum initial contribution: $0.00
Minimum Subsequent:	Minimum subsequent contribution: $0.00	Minimum subsequent contribution: $0.00
Max. Total Contribution:	Maximum total contribution: None	Maximum total contribution: $350,000.00
Investment Manager(s):	Multiple Investment Managers	Multiple Investment Managers

Data provided by College Savings Plan Network, an affiliate of the National Association of State Treasurers. Visit http://plans.collegesavings.org/planComparison.aspx for more information.

Alaska	Alaska 529	T. Rowe Price College Savings Plan	John Hancock Freedom 529
Plan Type(s):	Direct-sold	Direct-sold	Advisor-sold
Plan Website:	http://alaska529plan.com/	https://www3.troweprice.com/usis/personal-investing/products-and-services/college-savings-plans/t-rowe-price-college-savings-plan.html?van=collegesavings	http://www.jhinvestments.com/529
Plan Residency:	NO No state residency requirements.	NO No state residency requirements.	NO No state residency requirements.
State Tax Credit or Deduction?	NO Alaska does not have an income tax. Your state may offer tax deductions for contributions into Alaska 529.	NO Alaska does not have an income tax. Your state may offer tax deductions for contributions into the T. Rowe Price College Savings Plan.	NO Alaska does not have an income tax. Your state may offer tax deductions for contributions into the John Hancock Freedom 529 Plan.
State Tax Deferred Earnings/ Withdrawals?	YES Alaska does not have a state income tax; therefore, all earnings are exempt from taxes on earnings.	YES Alaska does not have a state income tax; therefore, all earnings are exempt from taxes on earnings.	YES Alaska does not have a state income tax; therefore, all earnings are exempt from taxes on earnings.
Financial Aid Benefits?	NO	NO	NO
State Matching Grants?	NO	NO	NO
Reward Programs?	NO	NO	NO
Direct-sold plan fees:	0.28% - 0.81%	0.41% - 0.83%	This is an advisor-sold plan.
Advisor-sold plan fees:	This is a direct-sold plan.	This is a direct-sold plan.	0.4% - 2.26%
Enrollment Fees:	$0	$0	$0
Investment Option Type(s):	Age-based, Blended, Capital Preservation, Equity, Fixed Income	Age-based, Blended, Capital Preservation, Equity, Fixed Income	Age-based, Blended, Capital Preservation, Equity ,
Min. Initial Contribution:	Minimum initial contribution: $0.00	Minimum initial contribution: $50.00	Minimum initial contribution: $250.00
Minimum Subsequent:	Minimum subsequent contribution: $0.00	Minimum subsequent contribution: $50.00	Minimum subsequent contribution: $50.00
Max. Total Contribution:	Maximum total contribution: $475,000.00	Maximum total contribution: $400,000.00	Maximum total contribution: $475,000.00
Investment Manager(s):	T. Rowe Price	T. Rowe Price	T. Rowe Price Associates, Inc.

Data provided by College Savings Plans Network, an affiliate of the National Association of State Treasurers. Visit http://plans.collegesavings.org/planComparison.aspx for more information.

Arizona	College Savings Bank	The Fidelity Arizona College Savings Plan	InvestEd
Plan Type(s):	Direct-sold	Direct-sold	Advisor-sold
Plan Website:	http://collegesavings.com/Arizona/	http://www.fidelity.com/arizona	http://www.waddell.com/
Plan Residency:	NO No state residency requirements.	NO No state residency requirements.	YES Fee waivers may be available to state residents.
State Tax Credit or Deduction?	YES Effective with the tax year beginning January 1, 2008, Arizona taxpayers can deduct contributions to a 529 college savings plan from Arizona State Income Taxes. Eligible individuals who are single/or designated as "head of household" can deduct up to $2,000 annually while married individuals filing jointly can deduct up to $4,000 annually.	YES Effective with the tax year beginning January 1, 2008, Arizona taxpayers can deduct contributions to a 529 college savings plan from Arizona State Income Taxes. Eligible individuals who are single/or designated as "head of household" can deduct up to $2,000 annually while married individuals filing jointly can deduct up to $4,000 annually.	YES Effective with the tax year beginning January 1, 2008, Arizona taxpayers can deduct contributions to a 529 college savings plan from Arizona State Income Taxes. Eligible individuals who are single/or designated as "head of household" can deduct up to $750 annually while married individuals filing jointly can deduct up to $1,500 annually.
State Tax Deferred Earnings/ Withdrawals?	YES Earnings on withdrawals used for qualified higher education expenses are not subject to State of Arizona income taxes. Arizona state income taxes are assessed on the earnings portion of any withdrawal that is not used for qualified higher education expenses.	YES Earnings on withdrawals used for qualified higher education expenses are not subject to State of Arizona income taxes. Arizona state income taxes are assessed on the earnings portion of any withdrawal that is not used for qualified higher education expenses.	YES Earnings on withdrawals used for qualified higher education expenses are not subject to State of Arizona income taxes. Arizona state income taxes are assessed on the earnings portion of any withdrawal that is not used for qualified higher education expenses.
Financial Aid Benefits?	YES Any student loan program, student grant program or other financial assistance program established or administered by this state shall treat the balance in an Arizona 529 Plan account of which the student is a designated beneficiary as neither an asset of the parent or the designated beneficiary nor as a scholarship, a grant or an asset of the student for determining a student's or parent's income, assets or financial need.	YES Any student loan program, student grant program or other financial assistance program established or administered by the State of Arizona shall treat the balance in an Arizona 529 plan account of which the student is a designated beneficiary as neither an asset of the parent of the designated beneficiary nor as a scholarship, a grant or an asset of the student for determining a student's or parent's income, assets or financial need.	YES Any student loan program, student grant program or other financial assistance program established or administered by this state shall treat the balance in an AZ 529 Plan account of which the student is a designated beneficiary as neither an asset of the parent of the designated beneficiary nor as a scholarship, a grant or an asset of the student for determining a student's or parent's income, assets or financial need.
State Matching Grants?	NO	NO	NO

Data provided by College Savings Plan Network, an affiliate of the National Association of State Treasurers. Visit http://plans.collegesavings.org/planComparison.aspx for more information.

Arizona (continued)	College Savings Bank	The Fidelity Arizona College Savings Plan	InvestEd
Reward Programs?	NO	**YES** Save more for college through everyday purchases with the Fidelity Investments 529 College Rewards American Express card. Customers earn 2 points for every dollar in net retail purchases charged to the card. Cards can be linked to eligible Fidelity 529 account(s).	Unknown
Direct-sold plan fees:	0%	0% - 1.06%	This is an advisor-sold plan.
Advisor-sold plan fees:	This is a direct-sold plan.	This is a direct-sold plan.	0.88% - 1.67%
Enrollment Fees:	$0	$0	$0
Investment Option Type(s):	Fixed Income, Guaranteed ,	Age-based, Blended, Capital Preservation, Equity, Fixed Income	Age-based, Blended, Equity, Fixed Income ,
Min. Initial Contribution:	Minimum initial contribution: $250.00	Minimum initial contribution: $50.00	Minimum initial contribution: $500.00
Minimum Subsequent:	Minimum subsequent contribution: $25.00	Minimum subsequent contribution: $25.00	Minimum subsequent contribution: $0.00
Max. Total Contribution:	Maximum total contribution: $431,000.00	Maximum total contribution: $350,000.00	Maximum total contribution: None
Investment Manager(s):	College Savings Bank	Fidelity Investments	Waddell & Reed

Arkansas	iShares 529 Plan	The Gift College Investing Plan
Plan Type(s):	Advisor-sold	Direct-sold
Plan Website:	https://www.ishares529.com/content/homel ogon.html	https://www.arkansas529.org/home.html
Plan Residency:	NO No state residency requirements.	NO No state residency requirements.
State Tax Credit or Deduction?	YES State tax deduction for Arkansas taxpayers — Arkansas taxpayers who contribute to The iShares 529 Plan can deduct up to $5,000 (up to $10,000 total for a husband and wife) from their Arkansas adjusted gross income for the year such contributions are made. This tax deduction applies to any contribution made on or after January 1 of each year. (Note that tax deductions will be added to a taxpayer's adjusted gross income in any subsequent year if the taxpayer rolls the account over to another state's 529 plan or if the taxpayer makes a non-qualified withdrawal.)	YES State tax deduction for Arkansas taxpayers — Arkansas taxpayers who contribute to The GIFT Plan can deduct up to $5,000 (up to $10,000 total for a husband and wife) from their Arkansas adjusted gross income for the year such contributions are made. This tax deduction applies to any contribution made on or after January 1, 2005. (Note that tax deductions will be added to a taxpayer's adjusted gross income in any subsequent year if the taxpayer rolls the account over to another state's 529 plan or if the taxpayer makes a non-qualified withdrawal.)
State Tax Deferred Earnings/ Withdrawals?	YES Tax-deferred growth and tax-free qualified withdrawals -- Any earnings in your GIFT Plan account grow federal income tax-deferred and earnings on your withdrawals are currently exempt from federal income tax when used for qualified higher education expenses.* The earnings portion of non-qualified withdrawals is subject to federal income tax and a 10% additional federal tax.	YES Tax-deferred growth and tax-free qualified withdrawals -- Any earnings in your GIFT Plan account grow federal income tax-deferred and earnings on your withdrawals are currently exempt from federal income tax when used for qualified higher education expenses.* The earnings portion of non-qualified withdrawals is subject to federal income tax and a 10% additional federal tax.
Financial Aid Benefits?	YES Arkansas offers a variety of financial aid programs through the Arkansas Department of Higher Education to help offset the cost of college in Arkansas.	YES Arkansas offers a variety of financial aid programs through the Arkansas Department of Higher Education to help offset the cost of college in Arkansas.
State Matching Grants?	NO	YES The Aspiring Scholars Matching Grant Program provides matching funds of up to $500 for up to five years for lower to moderate income families who meet the qualifications.
Reward Programs?	NO	YES Upromise is a free to join rewards program that can turn every day purchases — from shopping online to dining out, from booking travel to buying groceries — into cash back for college. A percentage of your eligible spending will be deposited into your Upromise account. You can link your Upromise account to your eligible 529 account and have your college savings automatically transferred. Visit Upromise.com/arkansas to learn more and enroll.
Direct-sold plan fees:	This is an advisor-sold plan.	0.43% - 57%
Advisor-sold plan fees:	0.35% - 1.3%	This is a direct-sold plan.
Enrollment Fees:	$0	$0
Investment Option Type(s):	Age-based, Capital Preservation, Equity, Fixed Income ,	Age-based, Blended, Capital Preservation, Equity, Fixed Income
Min. Initial Contribution:	Minimum initial contribution: $500.00	Minimum initial contribution: $25.00

Data provided by College Savings Plan Network, an affiliate of the National Association of State Treasurers. Visit http://plans.collegesavings.org/planComparison.aspx for more information.

Arkansas (continued)	iShares 529 Plan	The Gift College Investing Plan
Minimum Subsequent:	Minimum subsequent contribution: $50.00	Minimum subsequent contribution: $10.00
Max. Total Contribution:	Maximum total contribution: $366,000.00	Maximum total contribution: $366,000.00
Investment Manager(s):	BlackRock iShares	Ascensus Broker Dealer Services Inc., The Vanguard Group®

Colorado	CollegeInvest Direct Portfolio College Savings Plan	Scholars Choice College Savings Program
Plan Type(s):	Direct-sold	Advisor-sold
Plan Website:	https://www.collegeinvest.org/	http://www.scholars-choice.com/
Plan Residency:	NO No state residency requirements.	NO No state residency requirements.
State Tax Credit or Deduction?	YES Colorado taxpayers can deduct their contributions from their Colorado state taxable income up to their Colorado taxable income for that year, subject to recapture in subsequent years in which non-qualified withdrawals are made.	YES Colorado taxpayers can deduct their contributions from their Colorado state taxable income up to their Colorado taxable income for that year, subject to recapture in subsequent years in which a non-qualified withdrawal or rollover to a non-Colorado Section 529 plan is made.
State Tax Deferred Earnings/ Withdrawals?	YES Investments in any CollegeInvest Plan grow tax-deferred, and are free from federal and state income tax when used to pay for qualified higher education expenses.	YES Investments in any CollegeInvest Plan grow tax-deferred, and are free from federal and state income tax when used to pay for qualified higher education expenses.
Financial Aid Benefits?	YES At CollegeInvest, our goal is to be your trusted resource in providing 529 college savings plans to help everyone attain their higher education goals.	NO
State Matching Grants?	YES Middle- to lower-income families may qualify for a matching grant for contributions they make to a CollegeInvest account. Eligible participants can receive a $1 for $1 grant up to $400, for up to 5 years.	YES Middle- to lower-income families may qualify for a matching grant for contributions they make to a CollegeInvest account. Eligible participants can receive a $1 for $1 grant up to $400, for up to 5 years.
Reward Programs?	YES Upromise is a free to join rewards program that can turn every day purchases — from shopping online to dining out, from booking travel to buying groceries — into cash back for college. A percentage of your eligible spending will be deposited into your Upromise account. You can link your Upromise account to your eligible 529 account and have your college savings automatically transferred. Visit Upromise.com/colorado to learn more and enroll.	NO
Direct-sold plan fees:	0.36%	This is an advisor-sold plan.
Advisor-sold plan fees:	This is a direct-sold plan.	0.6% - 1.87%
Enrollment Fees:	$0	$0
Investment Option Type(s):	Age-based, Blended, Capital Preservation, Equity ,	Age-based, Blended, Capital Preservation, Equity, Fixed Income
Min. Initial Contribution:	Minimum initial contribution: $25.00	Minimum initial contribution: $250.00
Minimum Subsequent:	Minimum subsequent contribution: $15.00	Minimum subsequent contribution: $50.00
Max. Total Contribution:	Maximum total contribution: $400,000.00	Maximum total contribution: $400,000.00
Investment Manager(s):	Ascensus College Savings Recordkeeping Services, LLC., The Vanguard Group®	Legg Mason

Data provided by College Savings Plan Network, an affiliate of the National Association of State Treasurers. Visit http://plans.collegesavings.org/planComparison.aspx for more information.

Colorado	CollegeInvest Smart Choice College Savings Plan	CollegeInvest Stable Value Plus College Savings Plan
Plan Type(s):	Direct-sold	Direct-sold
Plan Website:	https://www.collegeinvest.org/	https://www.collegeinvest.org/
Plan Residency:	NO No state residency requirements.	NO No state residency requirements.
State Tax Credit or Deduction?	YES The CollegeInvest Smart Choice College Savings Plan is the only FDIC-insured option to include the state's income tax deduction. Colorado tax payers can deduct their contributions from their Colorado state taxable income up to their Colorado taxable income for that year, subject to recapture in subsequent years in which non-qualified withdrawals are made.	YES Colorado taxpayers can deduct their contributions from their Colorado state taxable income up to their Colorado taxable income for that year, subject to recapture in subsequent years in which non-qualified withdrawals are made.
State Tax Deferred Earnings/ Withdrawals?	YES Investments in any CollegeInvest Plan grow tax-deferred, and are free from federal and state income tax when used to pay for qualified higher education expenses.	YES Investments in any CollegeInvest Plan grow tax-deferred, and are free from federal and state income tax when used to pay for qualified higher education expenses.
Financial Aid Benefits?	NO	NO
State Matching Grants?	YES Middle- to lower-income families may qualify for a matching grant for contributions they make to a CollegeInvest account. Eligible participants can receive a $1 for $1 grant up to $400, for up to 5 years.	YES Middle- to lower-income families may qualify for a matching grant for contributions they make to a CollegeInvest account. Eligible participants can receive a $1 for $1 grant up to $400, for up to 5 years.
Reward Programs?	NO	NO
Direct-sold plan fees:	0%	0.71%
Advisor-sold plan fees:	This is a direct-sold plan.	This is a direct-sold plan.
Enrollment Fees:	$0	$0
Investment Option Type(s):	Guaranteed	Fixed Income
Min. Initial Contribution:	Minimum initial contribution: $0.00	Minimum initial contribution: $25.00
Minimum Subsequent:	Minimum subsequent contribution: $0.00	Minimum subsequent contribution: $25.00
Max. Total Contribution:	Maximum total contribution: $400,000.00	Maximum total contribution: $400,000.00
Investment Manager(s):	FirstBank	MetLife

Connecticut	Connecticut Higher Education Trust (CHET)	CHET Advisor
Plan Type(s):	Direct-sold	Advisor-sold
Plan Website:	http://www.aboutchet.com/	https://www.hartfordfunds.com/products/college-savings/chet-advisor.html
Plan Residency:	Unknown At this time, residency information has not been added for this plan.	YES Account owner must be state resident.
State Tax Credit or Deduction?	YES The amount contributed by a Connecticut taxpayer to CHET accounts during a tax year is deductible from Connecticut adjusted gross income in an amount not to exceed $5,000 for a single return or $10,000 for a joint return for that tax year. The Connecticut income tax deduction applies to contributions made in calendar year 2006 and beyond, including contributions dating back to January 1, 2006.	YES The amount contributed by a Connecticut taxpayer to CHET accounts during a tax year is deductible from Connecticut adjusted gross income in an amount not to exceed $5,000 for a single return or $10,000 for a joint return for that tax year. The Connecticut income tax deduction applies to contributions made in calendar year 2006 and beyond, including contributions dating back to January 1, 2006.
State Tax Deferred Earnings/ Withdrawals?	YES When you contribute to CHET, your account earnings have the opportunity to grow federal and Connecticut income tax-deferred until withdrawn. The earnings portion of any distributions used to pay for qualified higher education expenses will be free from federal and Connecticut income tax. This federal income tax-free treatment of qualified withdrawals and other federal tax benefits are now permanently in place for 529 plans through the passage of the Pension Protection Act of 2006.	YES When you contribute to CHET, your account earnings have the opportunity to grow federal and Connecticut income tax-deferred until withdrawn. The earnings portion of any distributions used to pay for qualified higher education expenses will be free from federal and Connecticut income tax. This federal income tax-free treatment of qualified withdrawals and other federal tax benefits are now permanently in place for 529 plans through the passage of the Pension Protection Act of 2006.
Financial Aid Benefits?	NO	NO
State Matching Grants?	NO	NO
Reward Programs?	Unknown	NO
Direct-sold plan fees:	0% - 1.12%	This is an advisor-sold plan.
Advisor-sold plan fees:	This is a direct-sold plan.	0.65% - 1.94%
Enrollment Fees:	$0	$0
Investment Option Type(s):	Age-based, Blended, Capital Preservation, Equity, Fixed Income	Age-based, Blended, Equity, Fixed Income, Guaranteed
Min. Initial Contribution:	Minimum initial contribution: $25.00	Minimum initial contribution: $50.00
Minimum Subsequent:	Minimum subsequent contribution: $25.00	Minimum subsequent contribution: $25.00
Max. Total Contribution:	Maximum total contribution: $300,000.00	Maximum total contribution: $300,000.00
Investment Manager(s):	TIAA-CREF	

Data provided by College Savings Plan Network, an affiliate of the National Association of State Treasurers. Visit http://plans.collegesavings.org/planComparison.aspx for more information.

Delaware

Delaware College Investment Plan

Plan Type(s):	Direct-sold
Plan Website:	http://www.fidelity.com/delaware
Plan Residency:	NO No state residency requirements.
State Tax Credit or Deduction?	NO
State Tax Deferred Earnings/ Withdrawals?	YES Delaware conforms to federal tax treatment
Financial Aid Benefits?	NO
State Matching Grants?	NO
Reward Programs?	YES Fidelity Rewards credit card linked to DCIP account offering 2.0% back into the DCIP account.
Direct-sold plan fees:	0.5% - 1.09%
Advisor-sold plan fees:	This is a direct-sold plan.
Enrollment Fees:	$0
Investment Option Type(s):	Age-based, Equity, Fixed Income
Min. Initial Contribution:	Minimum initial contribution: $50.00
Minimum Subsequent:	Minimum subsequent contribution: $25.00
Max. Total Contribution:	Maximum total contribution: $320,000.00
Investment Manager(s):	Fidelity Investments

District of Columbia

DC College Savings Plan

Plan Type(s):	Advisor-sold & Direct-sold
Plan Website:	http://www.dccollegesavings.com/
Plan Residency:	NO No state residency requirements.
State Tax Credit or Deduction?	YES Account owners who are District of Columbia residents may deduct up to $4,000 in plan contributions from D.C. taxes each year (up to $8,000 for married couples filing jointly if each taxpayer owns an account). D.C. residents who exceed the $3,000 contribution in a calendar year may carry forward and deduct the excess for up to 5 years.
State Tax Deferred Earnings/ Withdrawals?	YES All earnings on Section 529 college savings plans are exempt from District of Columbia taxation as long as distributions from the account are used to pay qualified higher education expenses.
Financial Aid Benefits?	YES The D.C. Tuition Assistance Grant Program allows District residents to attend any public college in the nation at in-state tuition rates. D.C. LEAP provides need-based grants of up to $5,000 per year to D.C. residents.
State Matching Grants?	NO
Reward Programs?	NO
Direct-sold plan fees:	0.15% - 1.97%
Advisor-sold plan fees:	0.5% - 1.97%
Enrollment Fees:	$0
Investment Option Type(s):	Age-based, Blended, Equity, Fixed Income, Guaranteed
Min. Initial Contribution:	Minimum initial contribution: $100.00
Minimum Subsequent:	Minimum subsequent contribution: $25.00
Max. Total Contribution:	Maximum total contribution: $260,000.00
Investment Manager(s):	Acacia Life Insurance Company, Calvert Investment Management, Inc., State Street Global Advisors

Florida	Florida Prepaid College Plans	Florida 529 Savings Plan
Plan Type(s):	Prepaid	Direct-sold
Plan Website:	http://www.myfloridaprepaid.com/	http://www.florida529plans.com/
Plan Residency:	YES Account owner or beneficiary must be state resident.	NO No state residency requirements.
State Tax Credit or Deduction?	NO Florida does not have a state income tax.	NO Florida does not have a state income tax.
State Tax Deferred Earnings/ Withdrawals?	NO Florida does not have a state income tax.	NO Florida does not have a state income tax.
Financial Aid Benefits?	NO	NO
State Matching Grants?	NO	NO
Reward Programs?	NO	NO
Direct-sold plan fees:	This is a prepaid plan.	0% - 0.75%
Advisor-sold plan fees:	This is a prepaid plan.	This is a direct-sold plan.
Enrollment Fees:	$50	$0 - $50
Investment Option Type(s):	Plan allows families to prepay certain higher education expenses, go to plan detail for more information.	Age-based, Blended, Capital Preservation, Equity, Fixed Income
Min. Initial Contribution:	Minimum initial contribution: $0.00	Minimum initial contribution: $25.00
Minimum Subsequent:	Minimum subsequent contribution: $0.00	Minimum subsequent contribution: $25.00
Max. Total Contribution:	Maximum total contribution: $0.00	Maximum total contribution: $418,000.00
Investment Manager(s):		AllianceBernstein Investments, Inc., Federated Investment Management Company, Fiduciary Management, Inc., Other - BMO Global Asset Management, PanAgora Asset Management, Inc., Quantitative Management Associates LLC, The Boston Company Asset Management, Wellington Management

Georgia — Path2College 529 Plan

Plan Type(s):	Direct-sold
Plan Website:	http://www.path2college529.com/
Plan Residency:	NO No state residency requirements.
State Tax Credit or Deduction?	YES All Georgia taxpayers may now contribute and deduct up to $2,000 each year for each beneficiary regardless of their annual income. Georgia taxpayers are not required to itemize deductions to make this adjustment to income. Please note that a transfer of funds from another state's 529 plan is not eligible for the Georgia income tax deduction. Georgia tax forms refer to the Path2College 529 Plan as "Georgia Higher Education Savings Plan" (GHESP); the Path2College 529 Plan is established by the GHESP. Contributions made during the tax year, or before the following year's federal tax filing deadline (generally April 15th) are eligible for the deduction. State tax benefits offered in connection with the Path2College 529 Plan are available only to Georgia taxpayers. You should consult with a qualified tax advisor regarding the application of Georgia state tax benefits to your particular circumstances. Recapture provisions may apply.
State Tax Deferred Earnings/ Withdrawals?	YES Contributions and earnings on any withdrawals used to pay for qualified higher education expenses will be free from federal and Georgia state income tax. The federal income tax-free treatment of qualified withdrawals and other federal tax benefits are permanently in place for 529 plans through the passage of the Pension Protection Act of 2006.
Financial Aid Benefits?	YES Assets in the Path2College 529 Plan are not considered as an asset of the parent, guardian, or student for purposes of determining an individual's eligibility for a need based grant, need based scholarship, or need based work opportunity offered or administered by any state agency except as may be required by the funding source of such financial aid. Georgia's HOPE scholarship program pays for tuition, fees, and provides a book allowance for students who graduate with a "B" average from an eligible high school. Other qualification criteria may apply.
State Matching Grants?	NO
Reward Programs?	NO
Direct-sold plan fees:	0% - 0.4%
Advisor-sold plan fees:	This is a direct-sold plan.
Enrollment Fees:	$0
Investment Option Type(s):	Age-based, Blended, Capital Preservation, Equity, Fixed Income, Guaranteed,
Min. Initial Contribution:	Minimum initial contribution: $25.00
Minimum Subsequent:	Minimum subsequent contribution: $25.00
Max. Total Contribution:	Maximum total contribution: $235,000.00
Investment Manager(s):	TIAA-CREF, TIAA-CREF

Hawaii

HI529-Hawaii's College Savings Program

Plan Type(s):	Direct-sold
Plan Website:	http://www.hi529.com/
Plan Residency:	NO No state residency requirements.
State Tax Credit or Deduction?	NO
State Tax Deferred Earnings/ Withdrawals?	YES Hawaii currently provides the same income tax treatment of contibutions made to the Program as the federal income tax treatment prior to December 31, 2002.
Financial Aid Benefits?	NO
State Matching Grants?	NO
Reward Programs?	YES Upromise is a free to join rewards program that can turn every day purchases — from shopping online to dining out, from booking travel to buying groceries — into cash back for college. A percentage of your eligible spending will be deposited into your Upromise account. You can link your Upromise account to your eligible 529 account and have your college savings automatically transferred. Visit Upromise.com/hawaii to learn more and enroll.
Direct-sold plan fees:	0.75%
Advisor-sold plan fees:	This is a direct-sold plan.
Enrollment Fees:	$0
Investment Option Type(s):	Age-based, Blended, Capital Preservation, Equity, Fixed Income
Min. Initial Contribution:	Minimum initial contribution: $15.00
Minimum Subsequent:	Minimum subsequent contribution: $15.00
Max. Total Contribution:	Maximum total contribution: $305,000.00
Investment Manager(s):	The Vanguard Group®

Idaho

IDeal - Idaho College Savings Program

Plan Type(s):	Direct-sold
Plan Website:	http://www.idsaves.org/
Plan Residency:	NO No state residency requirements.
State Tax Credit or Deduction?	YES Anyone who contributes regardless of account ownership and who is also an Idaho taxpayer can deduct up to $6,000 ($12,000 married filing jointly) annually from their state adjusted gross income for contributions.* * You will be required to include the entire amount of non-qualified distributions or transfers to another state's 529 plan in your Idaho taxable income. See the Enrollment Kit for full details.
State Tax Deferred Earnings/ Withdrawals?	YES Any earnings are Idaho and federally tax-free when used to pay for qualified expenses. Earnings on non-qualified withdrawals are subject to federal income tax and may be subject to a 10% federal penalty tax, as well as state and local income taxes. The availability of tax or other benefits may be contingent on meeting other requirements. See the Enrollment Kit for more details on qualified expenses.
Financial Aid Benefits?	NO
State Matching Grants?	NO
Reward Programs?	YES Upromise is a free to join rewards program that can turn every day purchases — from shopping online to dining out, from booking travel to buying groceries — into cash back for college. A percentage of your eligible spending will be deposited into your Upromise account. You can link your Upromise account to your eligible 529 account and have your college savings automatically transferred. Visit Upromise.com/idaho to learn more and enroll.
Direct-sold plan fees:	0.34% - 0.49%
Advisor-sold plan fees:	This is a direct-sold plan.
Enrollment Fees:	$0
Investment Option Type(s):	Blended, Capital Preservation, Equity, Fixed Income ,
Min. Initial Contribution:	Minimum initial contribution: $25.00
Minimum Subsequent:	Minimum subsequent contribution: $25.00
Max. Total Contribution:	Maximum total contribution: $500,000.00
Investment Manager(s):	Sallie Mae Bank, The Vanguard Group®

Data provided by College Savings Plan Network, an affiliate of the National Association of State Treasurers. Visit http://plans.collegesavings.org/planComparison.aspx for more information.

Illinois	College Illinois!® 529 Prepaid Tuition Program	Bright Directions College Savings Program
Plan Type(s):	Prepaid	Advisor-sold
Plan Website:	http://www.collegeillinois.org/	http://www.brightdirections.com/
Plan Residency:	YES Account owner or beneficiary must be state resident.	NO No state residency requirements.
State Tax Credit or Deduction?	YES Individuals subject to Illinois state income tax can deduct from their taxable income up to a maximum of $10,000 per year for contributions made toward the purchase of any College Illinois! Prepaid Tuition Program contract. Married couples filing jointly can deduct up to $20,000 per year. This state tax deduction reduces the individuals' adjusted gross income (AGI) by the amount contributed up to $10,000 (or $20,000 for those filing jointly). An annual statement sent by the program to account owners each year in January summarizes the contributions made during the tax year. Illinois tax form IL-1040 requires that Schedule M be attached to take the state tax deduction. The limit on the state tax deduction applies to combined contributions to the College Illinois! Prepaid Tuition Program, the Bright Start Savings programs, and the Bright Directions program.	YES Effective with the tax year beginning January 1, 2005, for each individual filer, up to a maximum of $10,000 in contributions ($20,000 if filing jointly) to the Program in a tax year is deductible from state taxable income for that tax year including the contribution portion of rollovers (but not the earnings portion of rollovers) from other Section 529 programs.
State Tax Deferred Earnings/ Withdrawals?	YES As long as benefits are used for education, the increased value of a College Illinois! Prepaid Tuition plan is 100% exempt from federal and Illinois state income tax.	YES Bright Direction account earnings are not taxed at the state or federal level.
Financial Aid Benefits?	NO	NO
State Matching Grants?	NO	NO
Reward Programs?	NO	YES The Bright Directions 529 College Savings Visa Rewards Card offers a 1.529% reward on everyday purchases
Direct-sold plan fees:	This is a prepaid plan.	This is an advisor-sold plan.
Advisor-sold plan fees:	This is a prepaid plan.	0.57% - 2.21%
Enrollment Fees:	$0	$0
Investment Option Type(s):	Plan allows families to prepay certain higher education expenses, go to plan detail for more information.	Age-based, Blended, Capital Preservation, Equity, Fixed Income
Min. Initial Contribution:	Minimum initial contribution: $0.00	Minimum initial contribution: $0.00
Minimum Subsequent:	Minimum subsequent contribution: $0.00	Minimum subsequent contribution: $0.00
Max. Total Contribution:	Maximum total contribution: $0.00	Maximum total contribution: $350,000.00
Investment Manager(s):	Selected by ISAC (Board)	American Century Investment Services, Inc., Ariel Capital, Barclays Global Investors, BlackRock, Calvert Group, Ltd.,, Delaware Investments, Dimensional Fund Advisors, Multiple Investment Managers, Multiple Investment Managers, NCM Capital Management Group, Inc, Northern Funds, Northern Trust Investments, N.A., OppenheimerFunds Inc., PIMCO, T. Rowe Price, William Blair

Illinois	Bright Start College Savings Program - Direct	Bright Start College Savings Program - Advisor
Plan Type(s):	Direct-sold	Advisor-sold
Plan Website:	http://www.brightstartsavings.com/	https://www.brightstartadvisor.com/
Plan Residency:	NO No state residency requirements.	NO No state residency requirements.
State Tax Credit or Deduction?	YES Effective with the tax year beginning January 1, 2005, for each individual filer, up to a maximum of $10,000 in contributions ($20,000 if filing jointly) to the Program in a tax year is deductible from state taxable income for that tax year including the contribution portion of rollovers (but not the earnings portion of rollovers) from other Section 529 programs.	YES Effective with the tax year beginning January 1, 2005, for each individual filer, up to a maximum of $10,000 in contributions ($20,000 if filing jointly) to the Program in a tax year is deductible from state taxable income for that tax year including the contribution portion of rollovers (but not the earnings portion of rollovers) from other Section 529 programs.
State Tax Deferred Earnings/ Withdrawals?	YES Bright Start account earnings are not taxed at the state or federal level.	YES Bright Start account earnings are not taxed at the state or federal level.
Financial Aid Benefits?	NO	NO
State Matching Grants?	NO	NO
Reward Programs?	NO	NO
Direct-sold plan fees:	0.18% - 0.69%	This is an advisor-sold plan.
Advisor-sold plan fees:	This is a direct-sold plan.	0.32% - 1.25%
Enrollment Fees:	$0	$0
Investment Option Type(s):	Age-based, Blended, Capital Preservation, Equity, Fixed Income, Guaranteed,	Age-based, Blended, Capital Preservation, Equity, Fixed Income, Guaranteed,
Min. Initial Contribution:	Minimum initial contribution: $25.00	Minimum initial contribution: $25.00
Minimum Subsequent:	Minimum subsequent contribution: $15.00	Minimum subsequent contribution: $15.00
Max. Total Contribution:	Maximum total contribution: $350,000.00	Maximum total contribution: $350,000.00
Investment Manager(s):	American Century Investment Services, Inc., Multiple Investment Managers, OFI Private Investments, Inc., The Vanguard Group®	American Century Investment Services, Inc., Multiple Investment Managers, OFI Private Investments, Inc. ,

Indiana	CollegeChoice 529 Direct Savings Plan	CollegeChoice Advisor 529 Savings Plan	CollegeChoice CD 529 Savings Plan
Plan Type(s):	Direct-sold	Advisor-sold	Advisor-sold & Direct-sold
Plan Website:	http://www.collegechoicedirect.com/	https://www.collegechoiceadvisor529.com/	http://www.collegechoicecd.com/
Plan Residency:	YES Fee waivers may be available to state residents.	YES Fee waivers may be available to state residents.	NO No state residency requirements.
State Tax Credit or Deduction?	YES Indiana residents can receive a 20% tax credit, up to $1,000 per year, on contributions into a CollegeChoice 529 Plan account.	YES Indiana residents can receive a 20% tax credit, up to $1,000 per year, on contributions into a CollegeChoice 529 Advisor Savings Plan account.	YES Indiana residents can receive a 20% tax credit, up to $1,000 per year, on contributions into a CollegeChoice 529 Plan account.
State Tax Deferred Earnings/ Withdrawals?	YES Earnings on qualified withdrawals are free from Indiana state income tax.	YES Earnings on qualified withdrawals are free from Indiana state income tax.	YES Earnings on qualified withdrawals are free from Indiana state income tax.
Financial Aid Benefits?	YES Indiana law provides that the amount of money that is available in a CollegeChoice 529 Investment Plan account and the proposed use of money in that account on behalf of a beneficiary, amy not be considered by the State Student Assistance Commission of Indiana when determining award amounts.	YES Indiana law provides that the amount of money that is available in a CollegeChoice 529 Investment Plan account and the proposed use of money in that account on behalf of a beneficiary, amy not be considered by the State Student Assistance Commission of Indiana when determining award amounts.	YES Indiana law provides that the amount of money that is available in a CollegeChoice 529 Investment Plan account and the proposed use of money in that account on behalf of a beneficiary, amy not be considered by the State Student Assistance Commission of Indiana when determining award amounts.
State Matching Grants?	NO	NO	NO
Reward Programs?	YES Upromise is a free to join rewards program that can turn every day purchases — from shopping online to dining out, from booking travel to buying groceries — into cash back for college. A percentage of your eligible spending will be deposited into your Upromise account. You can link your Upromise account to your eligible 529 account and have your college savings automatically transferred. Visit Upromise.com/indiana to learn more and enroll.	YES Upromise is a free to join rewards program that can turn every day purchases — from shopping online to dining out, from booking travel to buying groceries — into cash back for college. A percentage of your eligible spending will be deposited into your Upromise account. You can link your Upromise account to your eligible 529 account and have your college savings automatically transferred. Visit Upromise.com/ccadvsior to learn more and enroll.	NO
Direct-sold plan fees:	0.18% - 0.82%	This is an advisor-sold plan.	0%
Advisor-sold plan fees:	This is a direct-sold plan.	0.34% - 2.26%	0.00%
Enrollment Fees:	$0	$0	$0
Investment Option Type(s):	Age-based, Equity, Fixed Income, Guaranteed ,	Age-based, Equity, Fixed Income, Guaranteed ,	Guaranteed

Data provided by College Savings Plans Network, an affiliate of the National Association of State Treasurers. Visit http://plans.collegesavings.org/planComparison.aspx for more information.

Indiana (continued)	CollegeChoice 529 Direct Savings Plan	CollegeChoice Advisor 529 Savings Plan	CollegeChoice CD 529 Savings Plan
Min. Initial Contribution:	Minimum initial contribution: $10.00	Minimum initial contribution: $25.00	Minimum initial contribution: $25.00
Minimum Subsequent:	Minimum subsequent contribution: $10.00	Minimum subsequent contribution: $25.00	Minimum subsequent contribution: $25.00
Max. Total Contribution:	Maximum total contribution: $450,000.00	Maximum total contribution: $450,000.00	Maximum total contribution: $298,770.00
Investment Manager(s):	Ascensus College Savings Recordkeeping Services, LLC.	Ascensus College Savings Recordkeeping Services, LLC., Ascensus College Savings Recordkeeping Services, LLC.	College Savings Bank

Data provided by College Savings Plan Network, an affiliate of the National Association of State Treasurers. Visit http://plans.collegesavings.org/planComparison.aspx for more information.

Iowa	College Savings Iowa	Iowa Advisor 529 Plan
Plan Type(s):	Direct-sold	Advisor-sold
Plan Website:	http://www.collegesavingsiowa.com/	http://www.iowaadvisor529.com/
Plan Residency:	NO No state residency requirements.	NO No state residency requirements.
State Tax Credit or Deduction?	YES Iowa taxpayers can deduct up to $3,439 in contributions in 2020 (amount adjusted annually for inflation) per beneficiary from their state income tax. For example, a married couple with two children contributing to separate accounts can deduct up to $13,756 (that's 4 x $3,439) in 2020. If withdrawals are not qualified, the deductions must be added back to Iowa taxable income. Effective for tax years beginning on or after January 1, 2015, Iowa taxpayers may now elect to treat contributions to their College Savings Iowa account made up through the deadline (excluding extensions) for filing an individual Iowa state income tax return (generally April 30). Qualifying contributions are deducted on line 24, item "g." of your Iowa income tax return.	YES Iowa taxpayers can deduct up to $3,439 in contributions in 2020 (amount adjusted annually for inflation) per beneficiary from their state income tax. For example, a married couple with two children contributing to separate accounts can deduct up to $13,756 (that's 4 x $3,439) in 2020. If withdrawals are not qualified, the deductions must be added back to Iowa taxable income. Effective for tax years beginning on or after January 1, 2015, Iowa taxpayers may now elect to treat contributions to their IAdvisor 529 Plan account made up through the deadline (excluding extensions) for filing an individual Iowa state income tax return (generally April 30). Qualifying contributions are deducted on line 24, item "g." of your Iowa income tax return.
State Tax Deferred Earnings/ Withdrawals?	YES Earnings are fully exempt from Iowa state income tax. In addition, withdrawals are exempt from Iowa state income tax when used for qualified higher education expenses.	YES Earnings are fully exempt from Iowa state income tax. In addition, withdrawals are exempt from Iowa state income tax when used for qualified higher education expenses.
Financial Aid Benefits?	YES College Savings Iowa accounts are not included in determining eligibility for Iowa state financial aid programs. If you are not an Iowa resident, check with your state to determine its requirements.	YES College Savings Iowa accounts are not included in determining eligibility for Iowa state financial aid programs. If you are not an Iowa resident, check with your state to determine its requirements.
State Matching Grants?	NO	NO
Reward Programs?	YES College Savings Iowa offers a unique feature—the opportunity for you to add to your college savings with Upromise rewards. It's a free service that helps you earn money for college by giving back a percentage of what you spend with hundreds of America's leading companies. Upromise rewards makes saving for college easy.	NO
Direct-sold plan fees:	0.20%	This is an advisor-sold plan.
Advisor-sold plan fees:	This is a direct-sold plan.	0.83% - 2.36%
Enrollment Fees:	$0	$0
Investment Option Type(s):	Age-based, Blended, Capital Preservation, Equity, Fixed Income	Age-based, Blended, Capital Preservation, Equity, Fixed Income
Min. Initial Contribution:	Minimum initial contribution: $25.00	Minimum initial contribution: $250.00
Minimum Subsequent:	Minimum subsequent contribution: $25.00	Minimum subsequent contribution: $50.00
Max. Total Contribution:	Maximum total contribution: $420,000.00	Maximum total contribution: $420,000.00
Investment Manager(s):	The Vanguard Group®	Voya Investment Management

Kansas

	Learning Quest	Learning Quest Advisor
Plan Type(s):	Direct-sold	Advisor-sold
Plan Website:	http://www.learningquest.com/	http://www.learningquest.com/
Plan Residency:	NO No state residency requirements.	NO No state residency requirements.
State Tax Credit or Deduction?	YES Any contributor may deduct up to $3,000 for single filers and $6,000 for joint filers per beneficiary for contributions to any state sponsored 529 plan.	YES Any contributor may deduct up to $3,000 for single filers and $6,000 for joint filers per beneficiary for contributions to any state sponsored 529 plan.
State Tax Deferred Earnings/ Withdrawals?	YES follows federal treatment so that qualified withdrawals are tax free	YES follows federal treatment so that qualified withdrawals are tax free
Financial Aid Benefits?	NO	NO
State Matching Grants?	YES Kansas residents with household income lower than 200% of the federal poverty level ($48,600) for a family of four) can receive a match when they contribute at least $100 and up to $600.	YES Kansas residents with household income lower than 200% of the federal poverty level ($48,600 for a family of four) can receive a match when they contribute at least $100 and up to $600.
Reward Programs?	YES Account owners can link their Learning Quest accounts to their Upromise accounts.	YES Account Owners can link their Learning Quest Advisor accounts to their Upromise rewards account.
Direct-sold plan fees:	0.23% - 0.92%	This is an advisor-sold plan.
Advisor-sold plan fees:	This is a direct-sold plan.	0.48% - 2.56%
Enrollment Fees:	$0	$0
Investment Option Type(s):	Age-based, Blended, Capital Preservation, Equity, Fixed Income	Age-based, Blended, Capital Preservation, Equity, Fixed Income
Min. Initial Contribution:	Minimum initial contribution: $25.00	Minimum initial contribution: $25.00
Minimum Subsequent:	Minimum subsequent contribution: $0.00	Minimum subsequent contribution: $0.00
Max. Total Contribution:	Maximum total contribution: $370,000.00	Maximum total contribution: $370,000.00
Investment Manager(s):	American Century Investment Services, Inc., Robert W. Baird & Co., The Vanguard Group®	American Beacon Advisors, American Century Investment Services, Inc., Multiple Investment Managers, T. Rowe Price, The Principal Financial Group

Kansas	Schwab 529 College Savings Plan	KY Saves 529
Plan Type(s):	Direct-sold	Direct-sold
Plan Website:	http://www.schwab.com/529	http://www.kysaves.com/
Plan Residency:	NO No state residency requirements.	NO No state residency requirements.
State Tax Credit or Deduction?	YES Any Kansas taxpayer who contributes may deduct up to $3,000 for single filers and $6,000 for joint filers per beneficiary for contributions to any state sponsored 529 plan.	NO
State Tax Deferred Earnings/ Withdrawals?	YES follows federal treatment so that qualified withdrawals are tax free	YES Earnings are also exempt from Kentucky state income tax if used for qualified higher education expenses
Financial Aid Benefits?	NO	YES State Student Aid Eligibility - KESPT savings are not included in determining the amount of Kentucky state student need based aid a beneficiary will receive. However, other federal and institutional aid programs may take amounts in an account into consideration when determining eligibility.
State Matching Grants?	NO	NO
Reward Programs?	YES Account Owners can link their Schwab 529 accounts to their Upromise Rewards account.	NO
Direct-sold plan fees:	0.3% - 1.01%	0% - 0.91%
Advisor-sold plan fees:	This is a direct-sold plan.	This is a direct-sold plan.
Enrollment Fees:	$0	$0
Investment Option Type(s):	Age-based, Blended, Capital Preservation, Fixed Income ,	Age-based, Blended, Equity, Fixed Income, Guaranteed
Min. Initial Contribution:	Minimum initial contribution: $25.00	Minimum initial contribution: $25.00
Minimum Subsequent:	Minimum subsequent contribution: $0.00	Minimum subsequent contribution: $25.00
Max. Total Contribution:	Maximum total contribution: $365,000.00	Maximum total contribution: $350,000.00
Investment Manager(s):	American Beacon Advisors, American Century Investment Services, Inc., Baron Funds, Charles Schwab & Co. Inc., JP Morgan, Laudus Funds, Metropolitan West, Multiple Investment Managers, Robert W. Baird & Co., The Vanguard Group®	Other - Various

Kentucky	KY Saves 529	Kentucky's Affordable Prepaid Tuition
Plan Type(s):	Direct-sold	Prepaid
Plan Website:	http://www.kysaves.com/	http://www.getkapt.com/
Plan Residency:	NO No state residency requirements.	NO No state residency requirements.
State Tax Credit or Deduction?	NO	NO
State Tax Deferred Earnings/ Withdrawals?	YES Earnings are also exempt from Kentucky state income tax if used for qualified higher education expenses	YES Earnings are exempt from Kentucky state income taxes.
Financial Aid Benefits?	YES State Student Aid Eligibility - KESPT savings are not included in determining the amount of Kentucky state student need based aid a beneficiary will receive. However, other federal and institutional aid programs may take amounts in an account into consideration when determining eligibility.	YES KAPT accounts are not included when determining Kentucky state student financial aid program eligibility.
State Matching Grants?	NO	NO
Reward Programs?	NO	NO
Direct-sold plan fees:	0% - 0.91%	This is a prepaid plan.
Advisor-sold plan fees:	This is a direct-sold plan.	This is a prepaid plan.
Enrollment Fees:	$0	$50
Investment Option Type(s):	Age-based, Blended, Equity, Fixed Income, Guaranteed	Plan allows families to prepay certain higher education expenses, go to plan detail for more information.
Min. Initial Contribution:	Minimum initial contribution: $25.00	Minimum initial contribution: $0.00
Minimum Subsequent:	Minimum subsequent contribution: $25.00	Minimum subsequent contribution: $0.00
Max. Total Contribution:	Maximum total contribution: $350,000.00	Maximum total contribution: $0.00
Investment Manager(s):	Other - Various	State Street Global Advisors

Louisiana

Student Tuition Assistance and Revenue Trust (START) Saving Program

Plan Type(s):	Direct-sold
Plan Website:	http://www.startsaving.la.gov/
Plan Residency:	YES Account owner or beneficiary must be state resident.
State Tax Credit or Deduction?	YES Contributions to a START Saving Program Account are deductible up to $2,400 per beneficiary, per year, or, if married and filing jointly, $4,800 per beneficiary. Unused portions of the contribution limits may be carried forward to subsequent years.
State Tax Deferred Earnings/ Withdrawals?	YES Earnings on a START Saving Program Account are deferred until withdrawn and, if used for Qualified Higher Education Expenses, are tax exempt from Louisiana State income taxes.
Financial Aid Benefits?	YES The Value of an Education Savings Account has no impact on eligibility for Louisiana's scholarship programs.
State Matching Grants?	YES The State of Louisiana matches a portion of deposits to START accounts based on the Federal Adjusted Gross Income of the Account Owner and the Category of Account. Categories I through III are matched (2% to 14%) based on the account owner's AGI; Category 4 matches 2%; Category 5 has no state match since the beneficiary is not related and not a resident of Louisiana. Category VI accounts are matched (2% to 14%) based on the Federal Adjusted Gross Income of the Beneficiary's family.
Reward Programs?	Unknown
Direct-sold plan fees:	0% - 0.45%
Advisor-sold plan fees:	This is a direct-sold plan.
Enrollment Fees:	$0
Investment Option Type(s):	Age-based, Equity, Guaranteed
Min. Initial Contribution:	Minimum initial contribution: $10.00
Minimum Subsequent:	Minimum subsequent contribution: $10.00
Max. Total Contribution:	Maximum total contribution: $268,170.00
Investment Manager(s):	State Treasury, The Vanguard Group®

Data provided by College Savings Plans Network, an affiliate of the National Association of State Treasurers. Visit http://plans.collegesavings.org/planComparison.aspx for more information.

Maine	NextGen 529™ - Direct Series	NextGen 529™ - Select Series
Plan Type(s):	Direct-sold	Advisor-sold
Plan Website:	http://www.nextgenforme.com/	http://www.nextgenforme.com/
Plan Residency:	NO No state residency requirements.	NO No state residency requirements.
State Tax Credit or Deduction?	NO	NO
State Tax Deferred Earnings/ Withdrawals?	YES Maine is a tax conformity state.	YES Maine is a tax conformity state.
Financial Aid Benefits?	NO	NO
State Matching Grants?	YES As of 1/1/20, NextGen Initial Matching Grant Eligible Maine accounts opened and funded with a $25 contribution by 12/31/20 may receive a one-time $100 Initial Matching Grant, regardless of income. NextStep Matching Grant As of 1/1/20, The NextStep Matching Grant provides a 30% match on contributions, up to $300 per year, regardless of family income. Automated Funding Grant A $100 Automated Funding Grant is available for accounts that make at least six consecutive automated contributions through an automated funding option, regardless of income. Limit one per beneficiary.	YES NextGen Initial Matching Grant As of 1/1/2020, eligible Maine accounts opened and funded with a $25 contribution by 12/31/20 may receive a one-time $100 Initial Matching Grant, regardless of income. NextStep Matching Grant As of 1/1/20, the NextStep Matching Grant provides a 30% match on contributions, up to $300 per year, regardless of family income. Automated Funding Grant A $100 Automated Funding Grant is available for accounts that make at least six consecutive automated contributions through an automated funding option, regardless of income. Limit one per beneficiary.
Reward Programs?	NO	NO
Direct-sold plan fees:	0% - 0.53%	This is an advisor-sold plan.
Advisor-sold plan fees:	This is a direct-sold plan.	0% - 2.06%
Enrollment Fees:	$0	$0
Investment Option Type(s):	Age-based, Blended, Capital Preservation, Equity, Fixed Income	Age-based, Blended, Capital Preservation, Equity, Fixed Income
Min. Initial Contribution:	Minimum initial contribution: $25.00	Minimum initial contribution: $25.00
Minimum Subsequent:	Minimum subsequent contribution: $25.00	Minimum subsequent contribution: $25.00
Max. Total Contribution:	Maximum total contribution: $500,000.00	Maximum total contribution: $500,000.00
Investment Manager(s):	Bank of America, BlackRock, BlackRock iShares, Franklin Templeton Advisers, Inc., GIC and FDIC Insured Bank Deposit Account, MFS Investment Management	Allianz Global Investors Distributors LLC, American Century Investment Services, Inc., Bank of America-FDIC Insured Bank Deposit Account, BlackRock, BlackRock iShares, Eaton Vance, Franklin Templeton Investments, GIC and FDIC Insured Bank Deposit Account, Lord, Abbett & Co. LLC, MainStay Investments, MFS Investment Management, Neuberger Berman LLC, New York Life Insurance Company, New York Life Investment Management, OppenheimerFunds Inc., Thornburg Investment Management, Inc.

Maryland	Maryland Prepaid College Trust	Maryland College Investment Plan
Plan Type(s):	Prepaid	Direct-sold
Plan Website:	https://maryland529.com/college-savings-plans-of-maryland/maryland-prepaid-college-trust	https://maryland529.com/college-savings-plans-of-maryland/maryland-college-investment-plan
Plan Residency:	YES Account owner or beneficiary must be state resident.	NO No state residency requirements.
State Tax Credit or Deduction?	YES Each Account Holder, or an individual with Maryland taxable income who makes a contribution to a Maryland Prepaid College Tuition account, can deduct up to $2500 of payments each year from Maryland income per account. Payments above $2500 can be deducted in future years until the full amount of payments has been deducted.	YES Each Account Holder, or an individual with Maryland taxable income that contributes to a Maryland College Investment Plan account, can deduct up to $2500 of contributions each year from Maryland income per beneficiary. Contributions above $2500 can be deducted for up to the next 10 years.
State Tax Deferred Earnings/ Withdrawals?	YES Earnings are Maryland tax-free when used toward eligible college expenses.	YES Earnings are Maryland tax-free when used toward eligible college expenses.
Financial Aid Benefits?	NO	NO
State Matching Grants?	NO	NO
Reward Programs?	NO	NO
Direct-sold plan fees:	This is a prepaid plan.	0.38% - 0.83%
Advisor-sold plan fees:	This is a prepaid plan.	This is a direct-sold plan.
Enrollment Fees:	$75	$0
Investment Option Type(s):	Plan allows families to prepay certain higher education expenses, go to plan detail for more information.	Age-based, Blended, Capital Preservation, Equity, Fixed Income
Min. Initial Contribution:	Minimum initial contribution: $0.00	Minimum initial contribution: $25.00
Minimum Subsequent:	Minimum subsequent contribution: $0.00	Minimum subsequent contribution: $25.00
Max. Total Contribution:	Maximum total contribution: $0.00	Maximum total contribution: $350,000.00
Investment Manager(s):	College Savings Plans of Maryland Board, NA	T. Rowe Price

Massachusetts	The U.Plan Prepaid Tuition Program	The U.Fund College Investing Plan
Plan Type(s):	Prepaid	Direct-sold
Plan Website:	http://www.mefa.org/uplan	http://www.fidelity.com/ufund
Plan Residency:	NO No state residency requirements.	NO No state residency requirements.
State Tax Credit or Deduction?	YES U.Plan contributions can qualify you for a state income tax deduction of up to $1,000 for single filers, and up to $2,000 for married persons filing jointly.	YES Massachusetts residents saving in the U.Fund can claim a MA state income tax deduction of up to $1,000 for single filers and up to $2,000 for married persons filing jointly. Note your deduction on Schedule Y (the income modifications/deductions section on most tax software).
State Tax Deferred Earnings/ Withdrawals?	YES Invested in Municipal General Obligation Bonds	YES Earnings are state tax free when used for qualified higher education expenses.
Financial Aid Benefits?	NO	NO
State Matching Grants?	NO	NO
Reward Programs?	NO	YES Save more for college through everyday purchases with the Fidelity Investments 529 College Rewards American Express card. Customers earn 2 points for every dollar in net retail purchases charged to the card. Cards can be linked to eligible Fidelity 529 account(s).
Direct-sold plan fees:	This is a prepaid plan.	0.05% - 1%
Advisor-sold plan fees:	This is a prepaid plan.	This is a direct-sold plan.
Enrollment Fees:	$0	$0
Investment Option Type(s):	Plan allows families to prepay certain higher education expenses, go to plan detail for more information.	Age-based, Blended, Capital Preservation, Equity, Fixed Income
Min. Initial Contribution:	Minimum initial contribution: $300.00	Minimum initial contribution: $50.00
Minimum Subsequent:	Minimum subsequent contribution: $300.00	Minimum subsequent contribution: $25.00
Max. Total Contribution:	Maximum total contribution: $0.00	Maximum total contribution: $300,000.00
Investment Manager(s):	MEFA	Fidelity Investments

Data provided by College Savings Plan Network, an affiliate of the National Association of State Treasurers. Visit http://plans.collegesavings.org/planComparison.aspx for more information.

Michigan	Michigan Education Trust	Michigan Education Savings Program	MI 529 Advisor Plan
Plan Type(s):	Prepaid	Direct-sold	Advisor-sold
Plan Website:	http://www.setwithmet.com/	http://www.misaves.com/	http://www.mi529advisor.com/
Plan Residency:	YES Account owner or beneficiary must be state resident.	NO No state residency requirements.	NO No state residency requirements.
State Tax Credit or Deduction?	YES For lump sum purchases, the total contract price (including the processing fee) is eligible for the state tax deduction. For monthly purchase contracts, the total amount paid annually is eligible for the state tax deduction. See line 18 of the Michigan 1040 Schedule 1 form.	YES $5,000 for single tax filers and $10,000 for joint tax filers is eligible for the state tax deduction. See line 17 of the Michigan 1040 Schedule 1 form.	YES $5,000 for single tax filers and $10,000 for joint tax filers is eligible for the state tax deduction. See line 17 of the Michigan 1040 Schedule 1 form.
State Tax Deferred Earnings/ Withdrawals?	YES Michigan offers a state tax exemption on earnings if a MET contract is used to pay for qualified higher education expenses at a qualified higher education institution.	YES Michigan offers a state tax exemption on earnings if a MESP account is used to pay for qualified higher education expenses at a qualified higher education institution.	YES Michigan offers a state tax exemption on earnings if a MI 529 Advisor account is used to pay for qualified higher education expenses at a qualified higher education institution.
Financial Aid Benefits?	YES Michigan offers several financial aid benefits.	YES Michigan offers several financial aid benefits.	YES Michigan offers several financial aid benefits.
State Matching Grants?	NO	NO	NO
Reward Programs?	NO	NO	NO
Direct-sold plan fees:	This is a prepaid plan.	0% - 0.24%	This is an advisor-sold plan.
Advisor-sold plan fees:	This is a prepaid plan.	This is a direct-sold plan.	0.86% - 1.85%
Enrollment Fees:	$25	$0	$0
Investment Option Type(s):	Plan allows families to prepay certain higher education expenses, go to plan detail for more information.	Age-based, Blended, Equity, Fixed Income, Guaranteed	Age-based, Blended, Capital Preservation, Equity, Fixed Income
Min. Initial Contribution:	Minimum initial contribution: $25.00	Minimum initial contribution: $25.00	Minimum initial contribution: $25.00
Minimum Subsequent:	Minimum subsequent contribution: $14.00	Minimum subsequent contribution: $25.00	Minimum subsequent contribution: $25.00
Max. Total Contribution:	Maximum total contribution: $89,100.00	Maximum total contribution: $500,000.00	Maximum total contribution: $500,000.00
Investment Manager(s):	State Treasury, State Treasury	TIAA-CREF	Nuveen, TIAA-CREF

Data provided by College Savings Plans Network, an affiliate of the National Association of State Treasurers. Visit http://plans.collegesavings.org/planComparison.aspx for more information.

Minnesota	Minnesota College Savings Plan	Mississippi Affordable College Savings (MACS) Direct-Sold	Mississippi Prepaid Affordable College Tuition Program (MPACT)
Plan Type(s):	Direct-sold	Direct-sold	Prepaid
Plan Website:	http://www.mnsaves.org/	https://www.ms529.com/home.shtml	http://www.treasurerlynnfitch.ms.gov/collegesavingsmississippi/Pages/default.aspx
Plan Residency:	NO No state residency requirements.	NO No state residency requirements.	YES Account owner or beneficiary must be state resident.
State Tax Credit or Deduction?	YES Minnesota taxpayers may claim either a tax deduction or a tax credit depending on their income. A $1,500 tax deduction ($3,000 for a married couple filing jointly) can be claimed against Minnesota income tax. Alternatively, a tax credit equal to 50% of the contributions to accounts, reduced by any withdrawals, may be claimed with a maximum credit amount of up to $500, subject to a phase-out schedule starting at a federal adjusted gross income of $75,000.	YES (1) All property and income of the MACS Trust Fund, as an instrumentality of the state, is exempt from all taxation by the state and by its political subdivisions. (2) Any contributor or payor to a MACS Program account may deduct from their Mississippi taxable income any contributions or payments to an account or accounts in the MACS Trust Fund up to a maximum annual amount of Twenty Thousand Dollars ($20,000.00) for joint filers and Ten Thousand Dollars ($10,000.00) for single and other filers. Contributions or payments for such tax years may be made after such calendar years but before the deadline for making contributions to an individual retirement account under federal law for such years.	YES Tax Benefits - Payments you make for your child's MPACT plan are deductible for Mississippi income tax purposes. Earnings from MPACT are exempt from federal and state income tax. Consult your professional tax practitioner for detailed information.
State Tax Deferred Earnings/ Withdrawals?	YES Minnesota Revenue Notice # 00-09: Individual Income Tax – Taxation of Qualified State Tuition Programs Minnesota's income tax treatment of contributions and distributions from a qualified state tuition program under Internal Revenue Code § 529 follows the federal income tax treatment as to who, when, and how much money is includable in taxable income regardless of whether the program is the Minnesota College Savings Program established under Minnesota Statutes, section 136A.241 or another state's qualified tuition program. (See Minnesota Statutes, section 290.01,	YES The earnings portion of any withdrawals from an account that are not qualified withdrawals, as well as any amounts included in such nonqualified withdrawals previously deducted from taxable income under this section, shall be included in the gross income of the resident recipient of the withdrawal for purposes of the Mississippi Income Tax Law in the year of such withdrawal.	YES Tax Benefits - Payments you make for your child's MPACT plan are deductible for Mississippi income tax purposes. Earnings from MPACT are exempt from federal and state income tax. Consult your professional tax practitioner for detailed information.

Data provided by College Savings Plan Network, an affiliate of the National Association of State Treasurers. Visit http://plans.collegesavings.org/planComparison.aspx for more information.

	subdivision 19). Further, income is taxable by Minnesota only if the taxpayer reporting the income is a Minnesota resident at the time the income is recognized (Minnesota Statutes, section 290.17, subdivisions 1 and 2(e)) regardless of where the state program was established. Jennifer L. Engh Assistant Commissioner for Tax Policy Publication date: August 7, 2000 See: [link]		
Financial Aid Benefits?	NO	YES For any questions about Financial Aid Benefits offered in the State of Mississippi please contact: By Mail: Mississippi Office of Student Financial Aid 3825 Ridgewood Road Jackson, MS 39211-6453 By Email: sfa@ihl.state.ms.us By Phone: 1-800-327-2980	YES For any questions about Financial Aid Benefits offered in the State of Mississippi please contact: By Mail: Mississippi Office of Student Financial Aid 3825 Ridgewood Road Jackson, MS 39211-6453 By Email: sfa@ihl.state.ms.us By Phone: 1-800-327-2980
State Matching Grants?	NO	NO	NO
Reward Programs?	NO	NO	NO
Direct-sold plan fees:	0% - 0.33%	0% - 0.73%	This is a prepaid plan.
Advisor-sold plan fees:	This is a direct-sold plan.	This is a direct-sold plan.	This is a prepaid plan.
Enrollment Fees:	$0	$0	$60
Investment Option Type(s):	Age-based, Blended, Capital Preservation, Equity, Fixed Income, Guaranteed,	Age-based, Blended, Equity, Fixed Income, Guaranteed	
Min. Initial Contribution:	Minimum initial contribution: $25.00	Minimum initial contribution: $25.00	Minimum initial contribution: $0.00
Minimum Subsequent:	Minimum subsequent contribution: $25.00	Minimum subsequent contribution: $25.00	Minimum subsequent contribution: $0.00
Max. Total Contribution:	Maximum total contribution: $350,000.00	Maximum total contribution: $235,000.00	Maximum total contribution: $0.00
Investment Manager(s):	TIAA-CREF	TIAA-CREF	State Treasury

Missouri

MOST - Missouri's 529 College Savings Plan - Direct Sold

Plan Type(s):	Direct-sold
Plan Website:	http://www.missourimost.com/
Plan Residency:	YES Fee waivers may be available to state residents.
State Tax Credit or Deduction?	YES Your assets grow tax-deferred, and withdrawals are exempt from state income tax when used for qualified higher education expenses. Also, Missouri taxpayers can deduct up to $8,000 in contributions ($16,000 if married filing jointly) from their state income tax each year.
State Tax Deferred Earnings/ Withdrawals?	NO
Financial Aid Benefits?	NO
State Matching Grants?	NO
Reward Programs?	YES Upromise is a free to join rewards program that can turn every day purchases — from shopping online to dining out, from booking travel to buying groceries — into cash back for college. A percentage of your eligible spending will be deposited into your Upromise account. You can link your Upromise account to your eligible 529 account and have your college savings automatically transferred. Visit Upromise.com/missouri to learn more and enroll.
Direct-sold plan fees:	0.23% - 0.6%
Advisor-sold plan fees:	This is a direct-sold plan.
Enrollment Fees:	$0
Investment Option Type(s):	Blended, Capital Preservation, Equity, Fixed Income ,
Min. Initial Contribution:	Minimum initial contribution: $25.00
Minimum Subsequent:	Minimum subsequent contribution: $25.00
Max. Total Contribution:	Maximum total contribution: $235,000.00
Investment Manager(s):	The Vanguard Group®

Montana

Achieve Montana

Plan Type(s):	Direct-sold
Plan Website:	https://achievemontana.com/
Plan Residency:	NO No state residency requirements.
State Tax Credit or Deduction?	YES Montana residents are entitled to a $3,000 annual state tax deduction from gross income (married couples may deduct $6,000 per year). There is no recapture on withdrawals from accounts opened at least three years (you do not have to pay tax on your deductions upon withdrawal) if the contributions are used to pay qualified higher education expenses.
State Tax Deferred Earnings/ Withdrawals?	YES Qualified earnings distributed to pay higher education expenses are Montana tax free.
Financial Aid Benefits?	NO
State Matching Grants?	NO
Reward Programs?	YES Achieve Montana owners can register with the Upromise Rewards Program and earn cash-back rewards from numerous merchants and manufacturers. If linked to an Achieve Montana Plan account those rewards are periodically swept into the account to help maximize savings.
Direct-sold plan fees:	0.67% - 0.83%
Advisor-sold plan fees:	This is a direct-sold plan.
Enrollment Fees:	$0
Investment Option Type(s):	Age-based, Blended, Fixed Income
Min. Initial Contribution:	Minimum initial contribution: $25.00
Minimum Subsequent:	Minimum subsequent contribution: $15.00
Max. Total Contribution:	Maximum total contribution: $396,000.00
Investment Manager(s):	Dimensional Fund Advisors, First National Bank of Omaha, The Vanguard Group®

Data provided by College Savings Plan Network, an affiliate of the National Association of State Treasurers. Visit http://plans.collegesavings.org/planComparison.aspx for more information.

Nebraska	Nebraska Educational Savings Trust "NEST" Direct College Savings Plan	Nebraska Educational Savings Trust "NEST" Advisor College Savings Plan
Plan Type(s):	Direct-sold	Advisor-sold
Plan Website:	http://www.nest529.com/	https://www.nest529advisor.com/
Plan Residency:	NO No state residency requirements.	NO No state residency requirements.
State Tax Credit or Deduction?	YES Account owners that contribute to the NEST Direct Plan and file a Nebraska state income tax return are generally allowed to deduct up to $10,000 of contributions per year, per tax return ($5,000 per year if married filing separately), from their gross income for Nebraska state income tax purposes. This deduction also applies to the principal and earnings portions of rollovers from another state qualified college savings plan not issued by the State of Nebraska as well as amounts contributed after January 1, 2014 by custodians of an UGMA or UTMA account where the custodian is the parent/guardian of the Beneficiary of an UGMA or UTMA account (the "Parent/Guardian Custodian"). See "Part 14 – Federal and State Tax Considerations" for important additional information about state tax benefits.	YES Account owners that contribute to the NEST Advisor Plan and file a Nebraska state income tax return are generally allowed to deduct up to $10,000 of contributions per year, per tax return ($5,000 per year if married filing separately), from their gross income for Nebraska state income tax purposes. This deduction also applies to the principal and earnings portions of rollovers from another state qualified college savings plan not issued by the State of Nebraska as well as amounts contributed after January 1, 2014 by custodians of an UGMA or UTMA account where the custodian is the parent/guardian of the Beneficiary of an UGMA or UTMA account (the "Parent/Guardian Custodian"). See "Part 14 – Federal and State Tax Considerations" for important additional information about state tax benefits.
State Tax Deferred Earnings/ Withdrawals?	YES The earnings credited to an account will not be includable in computing the Nebraska taxable income of either the account owner or the Beneficiary of the account so long as the earnings remain in the account. There are no Nebraska state income taxes due on investment earnings paid out as a Qualified Withdrawal. However, there are Nebraska state income taxes due on investment earnings paid out as a Non-Qualified Withdrawal. The account owner or, after January 1, 2014 the Parent/Guardian Custodian, or Beneficiary will not be required to include any amount in computing Nebraska taxable income as a result of: (i) a permissible change of a qualifying Beneficiary of an account; or (ii) a transfer of amounts from an account of a Beneficiary to the account of a different qualifying Beneficiary, provided that in each case the new Beneficiary is a "Member of the Family" of the replaced Beneficiary and that the transfers occur either directly or by deposit to the new account within 60 days of the withdrawal from the prior account.	YES The earnings credited to an account will not be includable in computing the Nebraska taxable income of either the account owner or the Beneficiary of the account so long as the earnings remain in the account. There are no Nebraska state income taxes due on investment earnings paid out as a Qualified Withdrawal. However, there are Nebraska state income taxes due on investment earnings paid out as a Non-Qualified Withdrawal. The account owner, after January 1, 2014 the Parent/Guardian Custodian, or Beneficiary will not be required to include any amount in computing Nebraska taxable income as a result of: (i) a permissible change of a qualifying Beneficiary of an account; or (ii) a transfer of amounts from an account of a Beneficiary to the account of a different qualifying Beneficiary, provided that in each case the new Beneficiary is a Member of the Family of the replaced Beneficiary and that the transfers occur either directly or by deposit to the new account within 60 days of the withdrawal from the prior account.
Financial Aid Benefits?	YES The eligibility of the Beneficiary for financial aid may depend upon the circumstances of the Beneficiary's family at	YES The eligibility of the Beneficiary for financial aid may depend upon the circumstances of the Beneficiary's family at

	the time the Beneficiary enrolls in an Eligible Educational Institution, as well as on the policies of the governmental agencies, school or private organizations to which the Beneficiary and/or the Beneficiary's family applies for financial assistance. These policies vary at different institutions and can change over time. Therefore, no person or entity can say with certainty how aid programs, or the school to which the Beneficiary applies, will treat your account. However, financial aid programs administered by agencies of the State of Nebraska will not take your account balance into consideration, except as may be otherwise provided by federal law. For federal financial aid purposes, your account balance will be included in the calculation of your expected family contribution but only to the extent of approximately 5.64% of qualified assets.	the time the Beneficiary enrolls in an Eligible Educational Institution, as well as on the policies of the governmental agencies, school or private organizations to which the Beneficiary and/or the Beneficiary's family applies for financial assistance. These policies vary at different institutions and can change over time. Therefore, no person or entity can say with certainty how aid programs, or the school to which the Beneficiary applies, will treat your account. However, financial aid programs administered by agencies of the State of Nebraska will not take your account balance into consideration, except as may be otherwise provided by federal law. For federal financial aid purposes, your account balance will be included in the calculation of your expected family contribution but only to the extent of approximately 5.64% of qualified assets.
State Matching Grants?	NO	NO
Reward Programs?	YES If you are enrolled in the Upromise service, you can link that account to your NEST Direct Plan account and have all or a portion of your savings automatically transferred to your NEST Direct Plan from your Upromise Account on a periodic basis. The minimum amount for an automatic transfer made from a Upromise Account to your Plan account is $25. However, you cannot use the transfer of funds from a Upromise Account as the initial funding source for your Plan account. Transfers from a Upromise Account are not considered a deductible contribution for Nebraska state tax purposes.	YES If you are enrolled in the Upromise service, you can link that account to your NEST Advisor Plan account and have all or a portion of your savings automatically transferred to your NEST Advisor Plan from your Upromise Account on a periodic basis. The minimum amount for an automatic transfer made from a Upromise Account to your Plan account is $25. However, you cannot use the transfer of funds from a Upromise Account as the initial funding source for your Plan account. Transfers from a Upromise Account are not considered a deductible contribution for Nebraska state tax purposes.
Direct-sold plan fees:	0.2% - 1.26%	This is an advisor-sold plan.
Advisor-sold plan fees:	This is a direct-sold plan.	0.2% - 2.26%
Enrollment Fees:	$0	$0
Investment Option Type(s):	Age-based, Blended, Capital Preservation, Equity, Fixed Income, Guaranteed,	Age-based, Blended, Capital Preservation, Equity, Fixed Income, Guaranteed,
Min. Initial Contribution:	Minimum initial contribution: $0.00	Minimum initial contribution: $0.00
Minimum Subsequent:	Minimum subsequent contribution: $0.00	Minimum subsequent contribution: $0.00
Max. Total Contribution:	Maximum total contribution: None	Maximum total contribution: None
Investment Manager(s):	First National Bank of Omaha, First National Bank of Omaha, First National Bank of Omaha, First National Bank of Omaha	First National Bank of Omaha, First National Bank of Omaha

Nebraska	TD Ameritrade 529 College Savings Plan	The State Farm 529 Savings Plan
Plan Type(s):	Direct-sold	Advisor-sold
Plan Website:	http://collegesavings.tdameritrade.com/index.asp	https://www.statefarm.com/finances/education-savings-plans/state-farm-529-college-plans
Plan Residency:	NO No state residency requirements.	NO No state residency requirements.
State Tax Credit or Deduction?	YES Account owners that contribute to the Plan and file a Nebraska state income tax return are generally allowed to deduct up to $10,000 of contributions per year, per tax return ($5,000 per year if married filing separately), from their gross income for Nebraska state income tax purposes. This deduction also applies to the principal and earnings portions of rollovers from another state qualified college savings plan not issued by the State of Nebraska as well as amounts contributed after January 1, 2014 by custodians of an UGMA or UTMA account where the custodian is the parent/guardian of the Beneficiary of an UGMA or UTMA account (the "Parent/Guardian Custodian"). See "Part 14 – Federal and State Tax Considerations" for important additional information about state tax benefits.	YES Account Owners may deduct up to $10,000 in plan contributions from their federal adjusted gross income each year on their Nebraska tax return ($5,000 if married filing separately).
State Tax Deferred Earnings/ Withdrawals?	YES The earnings credited to an account will not be includable in computing the Nebraska (NE) taxable income of either the account owner or the Beneficiary of the account so long as the earnings remain in the account. There are no NE state income taxes due on investment earnings paid out as a Qualified Withdrawal. However, there are NE state income taxes due on investment earnings paid out as Non-Qualified Withdrawals. The account owner or, after January 1, 2014 the Parent/Guardian Custodian, or Beneficiary will not be required to include any amount in computing NE taxable income as a result of: (i) a permissible change of a qualifying Beneficiary of an account; or (ii) a transfer of amounts from an account of a Beneficiary to the account of a different qualifying Beneficiary, provided that in each case the new Beneficiary is a Member of the Family of the replaced Beneficiary and that the transfers occur either directly or by deposit to the new account within 60 days of the withdrawal from the prior account.	YES Earnings grow tax-deferred (which means your investment will accumulate faster because you are not paying taxes on it every year) "Withdrawals for qualified expenses are federally TAX-FREE and Nebraska State income tax-free. Financial Aid Benefits?YES Financial aid programs administered by agencies of the State of Nebraska will not take your account balance into consideration, except as may be otherwise provided by federal law. State Matching Grants? NO Reward Programs? NO Direct-sold plan fees This is an advisor-sold plan. Advisor-sold plan fees 0.2% - 0.61% Enrollment Fees $0 Investment Option Type(s) Age-based Blended Capital Preservation Guaranteed Minimum Initial Contribution Minimum initial contribution: $250.00 Minimum Subsequent Contribution Minimum subsequent contribution: $50.00 Maximum Total Contribution Maximum total contribution: $400,000.00 Investment Manager(s) First National Bank of Omaha First National Bank of Omaha First National Bank of Omaha First National Bank of Omaha
Financial Aid Benefits?	YES The eligibility of the Beneficiary for financial aid may depend upon the circumstances of the Beneficiary's family at the time the Beneficiary enrolls in an Eligible Educational Institution, as well as	YES The eligibility of the Beneficiary for financial aid may depend upon the circumstances of the Beneficiary's family at the time the Beneficiary enrolls in an Eligible Educational Institution, as well as on the policies of the governmental

	on the policies of the governmental agencies, school or private organizations to which the Beneficiary and/or the Beneficiary's family applies for financial assistance. These policies vary at different institutions and can change over time. Therefore, no person or entity can say with certainty how aid programs, or the school to which the Beneficiary applies, will treat your account. However, financial aid programs administered by agencies of the State of Nebraska will not take your account balance into consideration, except as may be otherwise provided by federal law. For federal financial aid purposes, your account balance will be included in the calculation of your expected family contribution but only to the extent of approximately 5.64% of qualified assets.	agencies, school or private organizations to which the Beneficiary and/or the Beneficiary's family applies for financial assistance. These policies vary at different institutions and can change over time. Therefore, no person or entity can say with certainty how aid programs, or the school to which the Beneficiary applies, will treat your account. However, financial aid programs administered by agencies of the State of Nebraska will not take your account balance into consideration, except as may be otherwise provided by federal law. For federal financial aid purposes, your account balance will be included in the calculation of your expected family contribution but only to the extent of approximately 5.64% of qualified assets.
State Matching Grants?	NO	NO
Reward Programs?	NO	NO
Direct-sold plan fees:	0.34% - 1.48%	0.34% - 1.48%
Advisor-sold plan fees:	This is a direct-sold plan.	This is a direct-sold plan.
Enrollment Fees:	$0	$0
Investment Option Type(s):	Age-based, Blended, Capital Preservation, Equity, Fixed Income	Age-based, Blended, Capital Preservation, Equity, Fixed Income
Min. Initial Contribution:	Minimum initial contribution: $0.00	Minimum initial contribution: $0.00
Minimum Subsequent:	Minimum subsequent contribution: $0.00	Minimum subsequent contribution: $0.00
Max. Total Contribution:	Maximum total contribution: $400,000.00	Maximum total contribution: $400,000.00
Investment Manager(s):	First National Bank of Omaha	First National Bank of Omaha

Nevada	Nevada Prepaid Tuition Program	SSGA Upromise 529 Plan
Plan Type(s):	Prepaid	Direct-sold
Plan Website:	http://nvprepaid.gov/	http://www.ssga.upromise529.com/
Plan Residency:	YES Account owner or beneficiary must be state resident.	NO No state residency requirements.
State Tax Credit or Deduction?	NO There are no state income taxes in Nevada	NO There are no state income taxes in Nevada
State Tax Deferred Earnings/ Withdrawals?	NO There are no state income taxes in Nevada	NO
Financial Aid Benefits?	NO	NO
State Matching Grants?	YES The Silver State Matching Grant program is offered through the SSgAUpromise 529 plan, not the Prepaid Tuition Plan.	YES Silver State Matching Grant Program launched March 1, 2010.If you qualify and are approved for the Program, contributions to your SSgA Upromise 529 account will be matched either dollar-for-dollar or one dollar-for-two dollars, up to $300 per year. There is a lifetime maximum of $1,500. Both you and the beneficiary must be Nevada residents You must be the account owner of a SSgA Upromise 529 Plan account. The beneficiary must be 13 or younger (when you are first approved for the matching grant) Your adjusted gross income must be $74,999 or less (see link below) If you qualify and are approved for the Program, contributions to your Upromise College Fund 529 Plan account will be matched either dollar-for-dollar or one dollar-for-two dollars, up to $300 per year. There is a lifetime maximum of $1,500.
Reward Programs?	NO	YES Upromise Rewards
Direct-sold plan fees:	This is a prepaid plan.	0.28% - 0.89%
Advisor-sold plan fees:	This is a prepaid plan.	This is a direct-sold plan.
Enrollment Fees:	$100	$0
Investment Option Type(s):	Plan allows families to prepay certain higher education expenses, go to plan detail for more information.	Age-based, Blended, Equity, Fixed Income ,
Min. Initial Contribution:	Minimum initial contribution: $0.00	Minimum initial contribution: $15.00
Minimum Subsequent:	Minimum subsequent contribution: $0.00	Minimum subsequent contribution: $50.00
Max. Total Contribution:	Maximum total contribution: $0.00	Maximum total contribution: $370,000.00
Investment Manager(s):	State Treasury	Sallie Mae Bank, State Street Global Advisors

Data provided by College Savings Plans Network, an affiliate of the National Association of State Treasurers. Visit http://plans.collegesavings.org/planComparison.aspx for more information.

Nevada	The Vanguard 529 College Savings Plan	Wealthfront 529 Plan
Plan Type(s):	Direct-sold	Advisor-sold
Plan Website:	https://personal.vanguard.com/us/whatwe offer/college/vanguard529?Link=facet	http://wealthfront.com/529
Plan Residency:	NO No state residency requirements.	YES Fee waivers may be available to state residents.
State Tax Credit or Deduction?	NO There are no state income taxes in Nevada	NO
State Tax Deferred Earnings/ Withdrawals?	NO	NO
Financial Aid Benefits?	NO	NO
State Matching Grants?	NO	NO
Reward Programs?	YES Upromise Rewards	NO
Direct-sold plan fees:	0.19% - 0.49%	This is an advisor-sold plan.
Advisor-sold plan fees:	This is a direct-sold plan.	0.00%
Enrollment Fees:	$0	$0
Investment Option Type(s):	Blended, Capital Preservation, Equity, Fixed Income ,	
Min. Initial Contribution:	Minimum initial contribution: $3,000.00	Minimum initial contribution: None
Minimum Subsequent:	Minimum subsequent contribution: $50.00	Minimum subsequent contribution: None
Max. Total Contribution:	Maximum total contribution: $370,000.00	Maximum total contribution: None
Investment Manager(s):	The Vanguard Group®	Wealthfront

Data provided by College Savings Plan Network, an affiliate of the National Association of State Treasurers. Visit http://plans.collegesavings.org/planComparison.aspx for more information.

New Hampshire	UNIQUE College Investing Plan	Fidelity Advisor 529 Plan
Plan Type(s):	Direct-sold	Advisor-sold
Plan Website:	http://www.fidelity.com/unique	http://advisor.fidelity.com/
Plan Residency:	NO No state residency requirements.	NO No state residency requirements.
State Tax Credit or Deduction?	NO New Hampshire does not have a personal income tax.	NO
State Tax Deferred Earnings/ Withdrawals?	YES New Hampshire does not have a personal income tax; qualified distributions are exempt from NH tax on interest and dividends	YES New Hampshire does not have a personal income tax; qualified distributions are exempt from NH tax on interest and dividends
Financial Aid Benefits?	NO	NO
State Matching Grants?	NO	NO
Reward Programs?	YES Save more for college through everyday purchases with the Fidelity Investments 529 College Rewards American Express card. Customers earn 2 points for every dollar in net retail purchases charged to the card. Cards can be linked to eligible Fidelity 529 account(s).	YES Credit Card Program that offers 2.0% rewards points. With the Fidelity Investments 529 College Rewards credit card, cardholders can earn points that automatically convert to Fidelity Advisor 529 Plan Account contributions.
Direct-sold plan fees:	0.05% - 1.04%	This is an advisor-sold plan.
Advisor-sold plan fees:	This is a direct-sold plan.	0.82% - 2.24%
Enrollment Fees:	$0	$0
Investment Option Type(s):	Age-based, Blended, Capital Preservation, Equity, Fixed Income	Age-based, Blended, Capital Preservation, Equity, Fixed Income
Min. Initial Contribution:	Minimum initial contribution: $50.00	Minimum initial contribution: $50.00
Minimum Subsequent:	Minimum subsequent contribution: $25.00	Minimum subsequent contribution: $50.00
Max. Total Contribution:	Maximum total contribution: $350,000.00	Maximum total contribution: $350,000.00
Investment Manager(s):	Fidelity Investments, Fidelity Investments	Fidelity Investments

Data provided by College Savings Plans Network, an affiliate of the National Association of State Treasurers. Visit http://plans.collegesavings.org/planComparison.aspx for more information.

New Jersey	Franklin Templeton 529 College Savings Plan	NJBEST 529 College Savings Plan
Plan Type(s):	Advisor-sold	Direct-sold
Plan Website:	https://www.franklintempleton.com/retail/pages/generic_content/home/splash_PUB/529-landing.jsf	https://www.njbest.com/njbest/enroll
Plan Residency:	NO No state residency requirements.	YES Account owner or beneficiary must be state resident.
State Tax Credit or Deduction?	NO Franklin Templeton 529 College Savings Plan is a federal and New Jersey state income tax-free investment for New Jersey residents. You won't owe federal or New Jersey state income tax on earnings for any assets that are withdrawn to pay for qualified education expenses.	NO Your investments in NJBEST grow federal income tax deferred and are federal income tax free if they're withdrawn to pay for qualified higher education expenses.
State Tax Deferred Earnings/ Withdrawals?	YES New Jersey offers state tax exemptions to New Jersey residents for qualified distributions from Franklin Templeton. Money invested in a 529 college savings plan grows federal income tax deferred and when withdrawn for qualified higher education expenses, earnings are free from federal income tax.	YES Your earnings in NJBEST grow federal income tax deferred and are federal income tax free if they're withdrawn to pay for qualified higher education expenses; you will not owe New Jersey state income taxes on earnings.
Financial Aid Benefits?	YES The first $25,000 of plan contributions will not be considered when determining a student beneficiary's eligibility for need based financial aid awarded by the state of New Jersey.	YES Financial aid break in New Jersey: New Jersey excludes $25,000 of your NJBEST 529 College Savings Plan from the student's financial need evaluation when determining eligibility for any scholarship, grant or other monetary assistance awarded by the state.
State Matching Grants?	NO	NO
Reward Programs?	NO	NO
Direct-sold plan fees:	This is an advisor-sold plan.	0.08% - 0.91%
Advisor-sold plan fees:	0.08% - 2.22%	This is a direct-sold plan.
Enrollment Fees:	$0	$0
Investment Option Type(s):	Age-based, Blended, Capital Preservation, Equity, Fixed Income	Age-based, Blended, Capital Preservation, Fixed Income ,
Min. Initial Contribution:	Minimum initial contribution: $250.00	Minimum initial contribution: $25.00
Minimum Subsequent:	Minimum subsequent contribution: $50.00	Minimum subsequent contribution: $0.00
Max. Total Contribution:	Maximum total contribution: $305,000.00	Maximum total contribution: $305,000.00
Investment Manager(s):	Franklin Templeton Distributors, Inc.	Franklin Templeton Investments

New Mexico	The Education Plan	Scholar'sEdge
Plan Type(s):	Direct-sold	Advisor-sold
Plan Website:	http://www.theeducationplan.com/	http://www.scholarsedge529.com/
Plan Residency:	NO No state residency requirements.	NO No state residency requirements.
State Tax Credit or Deduction?	YES New Mexico taxpayers may deduct the amount of contributions to an Education Plan account from their taxable income. There is an unlimited in-state tax deduction for contributions by New Mexico residents. However, the total deduction cannot exceed the cost of attendance at the applicable eligible higher education institution.	YES New Mexico taxpayers may deduct the amount of contributions to a Scholar's Edge account from their taxable income. There is an unlimited in-state tax deduction for contributions by New Mexico residents. However, the total deduction cannot exceed the cost of attendance at the applicable eligible higher education institution.
State Tax Deferred Earnings/ Withdrawals?	YES Earnings on withdrawals used for qualified higher education expenses are not subject to State of New Mexico income taxes. The State of New Mexico does not impose an additional penalty tax on the earnings portion of a non-qualified distribution. However, the deduction is subject to recapture upon a future non-qualified distribution.	YES Earnings on withdrawals used for qualified higher education expenses are not subject to State of New Mexico income taxes. The State of New Mexico does not impose an additional penalty tax on the earnings portion of a non-qualified distribution. However, the deduction is subject to recapture upon a future non-qualified distribution.
Financial Aid Benefits?	NO	NO
State Matching Grants?	NO	NO
Reward Programs?	NO	NO
Direct-sold plan fees:	0.25% - 70%	This is an advisor-sold plan.
Advisor-sold plan fees:	This is a direct-sold plan.	0.36% - 2.43%
Enrollment Fees:	$0	$0
Investment Option Type(s):	Age-based, Blended, Capital Preservation, Equity, Fixed Income	Age-based, Capital Preservation, Equity, Fixed Income ,
Min. Initial Contribution:	Minimum initial contribution: $25.00	Minimum initial contribution: $25.00
Minimum Subsequent:	Minimum subsequent contribution: $0.00	Minimum subsequent contribution: $25.00
Max. Total Contribution:	Maximum total contribution: $400,000.00	Maximum total contribution: $400,000.00
Investment Manager(s):	Dreyfus Corporation, OppenheimerFunds Inc., TIAA-CREF, Vanguard	American Century Investment Services, Inc., Dreyfus Corporation, MainStay Investments, New York Life Investment Management, OppenheimerFunds Inc.

New York	New York's 529 College Savings Program Direct Plan	New York's 529 Advisor-Guided College Savings Program
Plan Type(s):	Direct-sold	Advisor-sold
Plan Website:	http://www.nysaves.org/	https://www.ny529advisor.com/home
Plan Residency:	NO No state residency requirements.	NO No state residency requirements.
State Tax Credit or Deduction?	YES State income tax benefits. State income tax deduction of up to $5,000 ($10,000 for married couples filing jointly) for contributions if you are a New York State taxpayer.	YES State income tax benefits. State income tax deduction of up to $5,000 ($10,000 for married couples filing jointly) for contributions if you are a New York State taxpayer.
State Tax Deferred Earnings/ Withdrawals?	YES Earnings on qualified withdrawals are exempt from New York state income tax.	YES Earnings on qualified withdrawals are exempt from New York state income tax.
Financial Aid Benefits?	YES Under New York State law, assets in an Account are not taken into consideration in determining the eligibility of the Beneficiary or the Account Owner for financial aid under any New York State-administered financial programs, such as Tuition Assistance Program.	YES Under New York State law, assets in an Account are not taken into consideration in determining the eligibility of the Beneficiary or the Account Owner for financial aid under any New York State-administered financial programs, such as Tuition Assistance Program.
State Matching Grants?	NO	NO
Reward Programs?	YES Ascensus Broker Dealer Services, Inc., is the Program Manager for NYS 529 Program. You can add to your account in New York's 529 College Savings Program Direct Plan with Upromise® Rewards — you'll get free money for college when you spend with hundreds of America's leading companies.	YES Upromise is a free to join rewards program that can turn every day purchases — from shopping online to dining out, from booking travel to buying groceries — into cash back for college. A percentage of your eligible spending will be deposited into your Upromise account. You can link your Upromise account to your eligible 529 account and have your college savings automatically transferred. Visit Upromise.com/nya to learn more and enroll.
Direct-sold plan fees:	0.15%	This is an advisor-sold plan.
Advisor-sold plan fees:	This is a direct-sold plan.	0.65% - 2.15%
Enrollment Fees:	$0	$0
Investment Option Type(s):	Age-based, Blended, Capital Preservation, Equity, Fixed Income	Age-based, Blended, Capital Preservation, Equity, Fixed Income
Min. Initial Contribution:	Minimum initial contribution: $0.00	Minimum initial contribution: $1,000.00
Minimum Subsequent:	Minimum subsequent contribution: $0.00	Minimum subsequent contribution: $25.00
Max. Total Contribution:	Maximum total contribution: $375,000.00	Maximum total contribution: $375,000.00
Investment Manager(s):	Ascensus Investment Advisors LLC., The Vanguard Group®	JPMorgan Investment Advisors Inc., State Street Global Advisors

North Carolina

North Carolina's National College Savings Program

Plan Type(s):	Direct-sold
Plan Website:	http://cfnc.org/NC529
Plan Residency:	NO No state residency requirements.
State Tax Credit or Deduction?	NO
State Tax Deferred Earnings/ Withdrawals?	YES Account earnings are free from federal and, if you are a resident of NC, North Carolina income taxes when you use the money to pay for qualified higher education expenses.
Financial Aid Benefits?	NO
State Matching Grants?	NO
Reward Programs?	NO
Direct-sold plan fees:	0.25% - 0.39%
Advisor-sold plan fees:	This is a direct-sold plan.
Enrollment Fees:	$0
Investment Option Type(s):	Blended, Capital Preservation, Equity, Fixed Income, Guaranteed
Min. Initial Contribution:	Minimum initial contribution: $25.00
Minimum Subsequent:	Minimum subsequent contribution: $25.00
Max. Total Contribution:	Maximum total contribution: $450,000.00
Investment Manager(s):	State Employees' Credit Union, The Vanguard Group®

Data provided by College Savings Plans Network, an affiliate of the National Association of State Treasurers. Visit http://plans.collegesavings.org/planComparison.aspx for more information.

North Dakota | College SAVE

Plan Type(s):	**Advisor-sold & Direct-sold**
Plan Website:	http://www.collegesave4u.com/
Plan Residency:	**NO** No state residency requirements.
State Tax Credit or Deduction?	**YES** North Dakota taxpayers will be able to deduct up to $5,000 from their North Dakota state taxable income or up to $10,000 if married and filing jointly for their College SAVE contributions.
State Tax Deferred Earnings/ Withdrawals?	**YES** Earnings are fully exempt from North Dakota state income tax. Withdrawals are exempt from North Dakota state income tax when used for qualified higher education expenses at an eligible institution.
Financial Aid Benefits?	**YES** College SAVE accounts are not included in determining eligibility for North Dakota state financial aid programs. If you are not a North Dakota resident, check with your state to determine its requirements.
State Matching Grants?	**YES** North Dakota residents who open a new College SAVE account may be eligible for a single or multiple year matching grant from Bank of North Dakota of up to $300 per year. To be eligible for the grant, participants must meet certain requirements, including but not limited to: 1) The program matches up to $500 for singles earning $30,000 or less adjusted gross income (AGI); or $60,000 AGI or less if married, filing jointly. Account owners in this income group can apply for the match up to three years in a row. For account owners in a higher income bracket the program offers a one-time match of up to $500 for singles earning $60,000 AGI or less; or $100,000 AGI or less if married, filing jointly. 2) A participant must have made contributions to a College SAVE account within the 12 months of opening an account; 3) The account beneficiary (student) must be 15 years old or younger at the time of the matching grant application. and 4) The College SAVE 529 Matching Grant Application must be received no later than the end of the 13th month after opening the account and participants are required to attach a copy of their North Dakota state income tax return(s) to the Application.
Reward Programs?	**YES** Upromise is a free to join rewards program that can turn every day purchases — from shopping online to dining out, from booking travel to buying groceries — into cash back for college. A percentage of your eligible spending will be deposited into your Upromise account. You can link your Upromise account to your eligible 529 account and have your college savings automatically transferred. Visit Upromise.com/NorthDakota to learn more and enroll.
Direct-sold plan fees:	0.85%
Advisor-sold plan fees:	0.00%
Enrollment Fees:	$0
Investment Option Type(s):	Age-based, Blended, Capital Preservation, Equity, Fixed Income
Min. Initial Contribution:	Minimum initial contribution: $25.00
Minimum Subsequent:	Minimum subsequent contribution: $25.00
Max. Total Contribution:	Maximum total contribution: $269,000.00
Investment Manager(s):	The Vanguard Group®

Ohio	CollegeAdvantage Direct 529 Savings Plan	CollegeAdvantage Advisor 529, offered by BlackRock
Plan Type(s):	Direct-sold	Advisor-sold
Plan Website:	https://www.collegeadvantage.com/	http://www.blackrock.com/collegeadvantage
Plan Residency:	NO No state residency requirements.	NO No state residency requirements.
State Tax Credit or Deduction?	YES Ohio taxpayers may deduct their contributions to a CollegeAdvantage account from Ohio taxable income. Each contributor (or married couple) may deduct contributions up to $4,000 per beneficiary, per calendar year, with unlimited carry forward in future years. Non-account owners who make contributions to a CollegeAdvantage account and are Ohio taxpayers, may also take the Ohio income tax deduction, subject to the same limitations as account owners.	YES Ohio taxpayers can deduct their contributions to a CollegeAdvantage account from Ohio taxable income. Each contributor (or married couple) can deduct up to $4,000 per beneficiary, per calendar year, with unlimited carry forward in future years.
State Tax Deferred Earnings/ Withdrawals?	YES Earnings on withdrawals used for qualified higher education expenses are not subject to State of Ohio income taxes. State of Ohio income taxes are assessed on the earnings portion of any withdrawal that is not used for qualified higher education expenses.	YES Earnings on withdrawals used for qualified higher education expenses are not subject to State of Ohio income taxes. Ohio state income taxes are assessed on the earnings portion of any withdrawal that is not used for qualified higher education expenses.
Financial Aid Benefits?	NO	NO
State Matching Grants?	NO	NO
Reward Programs?	YES CollegeAdvantage Direct Plan Account Owners may link their Upromise account to their Direct Plan account(s). Upromise is free to join and can help you earn cash back for college on everyday purchases like online shopping, dining out, buying groceries, booking hotels and travel and so much more. When you join Upromise, you can link your Upromise account to your CollegeAdvantage Direct 529 Plan account so your Upromise earnings can be transferred automatically to your CollegeAdvantage Direct Plan account on a periodic basis.	NO
Direct-sold plan fees:	0% - 0.53%	This is an advisor-sold plan.
Advisor-sold plan fees:	This is a direct-sold plan.	0.53% - 1.76%
Enrollment Fees:	$0	$0
Investment Option Type(s):	Age-based, Blended, Capital Preservation, Equity, Fixed Income	Age-based, Blended, Equity, Fixed Income ,
Min. Initial Contribution:	Minimum initial contribution: $25.00	Minimum initial contribution: $25.00
Minimum Subsequent:	Minimum subsequent contribution: $25.00	Minimum subsequent contribution: $25.00
Max. Total Contribution:	Maximum total contribution: $462,000.00	Maximum total contribution: $426,000.00
Investment Manager(s):	Dimensional Fund Advisors, Fifth Third Bank, Ohio Tuition Trust Authority, The Vanguard Group®	BlackRock, BlackRock iShares, Voya Investment Management, Wells Fargo Funds Management, LLC

Oklahoma	Oklahoma College Savings Plan	OklahomaDream 529 Plan
Plan Type(s):	Direct-sold	Advisor-sold
Plan Website:	http://www.ok4saving.org/	http://www.okdream529.com/
Plan Residency:	NO No state residency requirements.	NO No state residency requirements.
State Tax Credit or Deduction?	YES Deduction of $10,000 individual or $20,000 per married couple per year; Earnings are exempt.	YES Contributions to the OklahomaDream 529 Plan, including rollover contributions, of up to $10,000 per year for an individual taxpayer, and up to $20,000 per year for a married couple filing jointly, are deductible in computing Oklahoma taxable income, with a five-year carryforward of excess contributions. Contribution deadline is April 15th of the following year.
State Tax Deferred Earnings/ Withdrawals?	YES The earnings portion of any distributions used to pay for qualified higher education expenses will be free from federal and Oklahoma income tax.	YES Oklahoma offers a state tax exemption on earnings if an OklahomaDream 529 Plan account is used to pay for qualified higher education expenses.
Financial Aid Benefits?	NO	NO
State Matching Grants?	NO	NO
Reward Programs?	NO	NO
Direct-sold plan fees:	0% - 0.78%	This is an advisor-sold plan.
Advisor-sold plan fees:	This is a direct-sold plan.	0.81% - 2.44%
Enrollment Fees:	$0	$0
Investment Option Type(s):	Age-based, Blended, Equity, Fixed Income, Guaranteed	Age-based, Blended, Capital Preservation, Equity, Fixed Income
Min. Initial Contribution:	Minimum initial contribution: $0.00	Minimum initial contribution: $1,000.00
Minimum Subsequent:	Minimum subsequent contribution: $0.00	Minimum subsequent contribution: $25.00
Max. Total Contribution:	Maximum total contribution: None	Maximum total contribution: $300,000.00
Investment Manager(s):	TIAA-CREF	Allianz Global Investors Distributors LLC, PIMCO, TIAA-CREF

Data provided by College Savings Plan Network, an affiliate of the National Association of State Treasurers. Visit http://plans.collegesavings.org/planComparison.aspx for more information.

Oregon	Oregon College Savings Plan	MFS 529 Savings Plan
Plan Type(s):	Direct-sold	Advisor-sold
Plan Website:	http://www.oregoncollegesavings.com/	https://www.mfs.com/en-us/individual-investor/planning-for-the-future.html?tabname=529-college-planning
Plan Residency:	NO No state residency requirements.	NO No state residency requirements.
State Tax Credit or Deduction?	YES All Oregon taxpayers are eligible to receive a state income tax credit up to $300 for joint filers and up to $150 for single filers on contributions made to their Oregon College Savings Plan account. The tax credit goes into effect on January 1, 2020, replacing the state income tax deduction, and provides the same maximum credit to all Oregonians who are saving for college, community college, trade school, or any other post-secondary education through the Oregon College Savings Plan.	YES All Oregon taxpayers are eligible to receive a state income tax credit up to $300 for joint filers and up to $150 for single filers on contributions made to their MFS 529 Savings Plan account. The tax credit goes into effect on January 1, 2020, replacing the state income tax deduction, and provides the same maximum credit to all Oregonians who are saving for college, community college, trade school, or any other post-secondary education through the MFS 529 Savings Plan.
State Tax Deferred Earnings/ Withdrawals?	YES All earnings are state tax exempt if used for qualified higher education expenses.	YES All earnings are state tax exempt if used for qualified expenses.
Financial Aid Benefits?	NO	NO
State Matching Grants?	NO	NO
Reward Programs?	NO	NO
Direct-sold plan fees:	0% - 0.7%	This is an advisor-sold plan.
Advisor-sold plan fees:	This is a direct-sold plan.	0.74% - 2.25%
Enrollment Fees:	$0	$0
Investment Option Type(s):	Age-based, Blended, Capital Preservation, Equity, Fixed Income, Guaranteed,	Age-based, Blended, Capital Preservation, Equity, Fixed Income
Min. Initial Contribution:	Minimum initial contribution: $25.00	Minimum initial contribution: $250.00
Minimum Subsequent:	Minimum subsequent contribution: $25.00	Minimum subsequent contribution: $0.00
Max. Total Contribution:	Maximum total contribution: $310,000.00	Maximum total contribution: $310,000.00
Investment Manager(s):	Sumday, a division of BNY Mellon	MFS Investment Management

Data provided by College Savings Plans Network, an affiliate of the National Association of State Treasurers. Visit http://plans.collegesavings.org/planComparison.aspx for more information.

Pennsylvania	Pennsylvania 529 Guaranteed Savings Plan	Pennsylvania 529 Investment Plan
Plan Type(s):	Prepaid	Direct-sold
Plan Website:	http://www.pa529.com/	http://www.pa529.com/
Plan Residency:	YES Account owner or beneficiary must be state resident.	NO No state residency requirements.
State Tax Credit or Deduction?	YES For individuals subject to Pennsylvania income tax, contributions made to an account may be deducted from taxable income on the taxpayer's annual personal income tax return. The maximum annual amount that may be deducted is currently $15,000 per beneficiary per taxpayer but that amount will increase with any changes in the amount excludable for federal gift tax purposes. The deduction cannot result in the taxable income being less than zero. The new state law also provides that the earnings portion of any Qualified Withdrawal is exempt from Pennsylvania income tax.	YES For individuals subject to Pennsylvania income tax, contributions made to an account may be deducted from taxable income on the taxpayer's annual personal income tax return. The maximum annual amount that may be deducted is currently $15,000 per beneficiary per taxpayer but that amount will increase with any changes in the amount excludable for federal gift tax purposes. The deduction cannot result in the taxable income being less than zero. State law also provides that the earnings portion of any Qualified Withdrawal is exempt from Pennsylvania income tax.
State Tax Deferred Earnings/ Withdrawals?	YES The earnings portion of any Qualified Withdrawal is exempt from Pennsylvania income tax. Non-Qualified Withdrawals are subjected to Pennsylvania income tax.	YES The earnings portion of any Qualified Withdrawal is exempt from Pennsylvania income tax. Non-Qualified Withdrawals are subjected to Pennsylvania income tax.
Financial Aid Benefits?	YES Pennsylvania law expressly provides that a PA 529 GSP Account may not have any effect on eligibility for state financial aid. Such aid would primarily be state grant programs administered by the Pennsylvania Higher Education Assistance Agency ("PHEAA"). Financial aid rules are subject to change. The procedures and rules in effect when a Beneficiary applies for aid may be different than those described above.	YES Pennsylvania law expressly provides that a PA 529 IP Account may not have any effect on eligibility for state financial aid. Such aid would primarily be state grant programs administered by the Pennsylvania Higher Education Assistance Agency ("PHEAA"). Financial aid rules are subject to change. The procedures and rules in effect when a Beneficiary applies for aid may be different than those described above.
State Matching Grants?	NO	NO
Reward Programs?	YES Upromise Service Upromise Service is a free rewards service that lets members get back a percentage of their qualified spending with hundreds of America's leading companies as college savings. Once you enroll in the PA 529 GSP, your Upromise account and your PA 529 GSP account can be linked so that your rebate dollars are automatically transferred to your PA 529 GSP account on a periodic basis.	YES Upromise Service Upromise Service is a free rewards service that lets members get back a percentage of their qualified spending with hundreds of America's leading companies as college savings. Once you enroll in the PA 529 IP, your Upromise account and your PA 529 IP account can be linked so that your rebate dollars are automatically transferred to your PA 529 IP account on a periodic basis.
Direct-sold plan fees:	This is a prepaid plan.	0.215% - 0.315%
Advisor-sold plan fees:	This is a prepaid plan.	This is a direct-sold plan.
Enrollment Fees:	$50	$0
Investment Option Type(s):	Not applicable, go to plan detail for more information.	Age-based, Blended, Capital Preservation, Equity, Fixed Income
Min. Initial Contribution:	Minimum initial contribution: $15.00	Minimum initial contribution: $25.00
Minimum Subsequent:	Minimum subsequent contribution: $15.00	Minimum subsequent contribution: $25.00
Max. Total Contribution:	Maximum total contribution: $511,758.00	Maximum total contribution: $511,758.00
Investment Manager(s):	Pennsylvania Treasury Department	The Vanguard Group®

Data provided by College Savings Plan Network, an affiliate of the National Association of State Treasurers. Visit http://plans.collegesavings.org/planComparison.aspx for more information.

Rhode Island

CollegeBound 529

Plan Type(s):	Advisor-sold
Plan Website:	http://www.collegebound529.com/
Plan Residency:	NO No state residency requirements.
State Tax Credit or Deduction?	YES Rhode Island taxpayers who are account owners are eligible for a deduction in computing state income tax of up to $1,000 for married couples filing jointly and $500 for individual filers for contributions to their CollegeBound 529account married couple filing jointly (up to $500 for a single filer).
State Tax Deferred Earnings/ Withdrawals?	YES Earnings grow tax deferred from federal and state taxes. Distributions for qualified expenses are exempt from federal and state tax.
Financial Aid Benefits?	NO
State Matching Grants?	NO
Reward Programs?	YES Upromise is a rewards program that believes everyone should have a chance to go to college and pursue his or her dreams. Since 2001, Upromise has helped its members earn millions in cash back for college from eligible purchases you most likely make every day. Here's how it works: Join Upromise for free and then do what you normally do—buy groceries, shop online, book travel, dine at restaurants, and more—through participating partners. A percentage of your eligible spending will be deposited in your Upromise account. Signing up is fast, easy, and secure. You can easily link your Upromise account with your eligible 529 account and have your college savings automatically transferred into your CollegeBound 529 account.
Direct-sold plan fees:	This is an advisor-sold plan.
Advisor-sold plan fees:	0.19% - 1.7%
Enrollment Fees:	$0
Investment Option Type(s):	Age-based
Min. Initial Contribution:	Minimum initial contribution: $0.00
Minimum Subsequent:	Minimum subsequent contribution: $0.00
Max. Total Contribution:	Maximum total contribution: None
Investment Manager(s):	Invesco

South Carolina	SC Tuition Prepayment Program (SCTPP)	Future Scholar 529 College Savings Plan - Direct Investment Program	Future Scholar 529 College Savings Plan - Advisor Program
Plan Type(s):	Prepaid	Direct-sold	Advisor-sold
Plan Website:	http://www.scprepaid.com/home.aspx	https://futurescholar.com/	https://futurescholar.com/
Plan Residency:	YES Account owner or beneficiary must be state resident.	YES Account owner or beneficiary must be state resident.	NO No state residency requirements.
State Tax Credit or Deduction?	YES Contributors may claim the amount of contributions made to any SCTPP accounts when they use the SC 1040 Long Form.	YES Contributions are deductible in computing the contributor's South Carolina taxable income for South Carolina personal income tax purposes.	YES Contributions are deductible in computing the contributor's South Carolina taxable income for South Carolina personal income tax purposes.
State Tax Deferred Earnings/ Withdrawals?	YES SC complies with the federal tax exemption on earnings.	YES SC complies with the federal tax exemption on earnings.	YES SC complies with the federal tax exemption on earnings.
Financial Aid Benefits?	NO	YES Available balances in a Section 529 Program account will be treated as an asset of (a) the student if the student is an independent student or (b) the parent if the student is a dependent student, regardless of whether the owner of the Section 529 Program account is the student or the parent.	YES Available balances in a Section 529 Program account will be treated as an asset of (a) the student if the student is an independent student or (b) the parent if the student is a dependent student, regardless of whether the owner of the Section 529 Program account is the student or the parent.
State Matching Grants?	NO	NO	NO
Reward Programs?	NO	NO	NO
Direct-sold plan fees:	This is a prepaid plan.	0% - 0.24%	This is an advisor-sold plan.
Advisor-sold plan fees:	This is a prepaid plan.	This is a direct-sold plan.	0% - 2.17%
Enrollment Fees:	$0	$0	$0
Investment Option Type(s):		Age-based, Blended, Capital Preservation, Equity, Fixed Income	Age-based, Blended, Capital Preservation, Equity, Fixed Income
Min. Initial Contribution:	Minimum initial contribution: $0.00	Minimum initial contribution: $0.00	Minimum initial contribution: $100.00
Minimum Subsequent:	Minimum subsequent contribution: $0.00	Minimum subsequent contribution: $0.00	Minimum subsequent contribution: $25.00
Max. Total Contribution:	Maximum total contribution: $0.00	Maximum total contribution: None	Maximum total contribution: $500,000.00
Investment Manager(s):	SC Office of State Treasurer, Curtis M. Loftis, Jr.	Columbia Management Group, LLC	Columbia Management Group, LLC

Data provided by College Savings Plan Network, an affiliate of the National Association of State Treasurers. Visit http://plans.collegesavings.org/planComparison.aspx for more information.

South Dakota

CollegeAccess 529

Plan Type(s):	**Advisor-sold & Direct-sold**
Plan Website:	http://www.collegeaccess529.com/
Plan Residency:	NO No state residency requirements.
State Tax Credit or Deduction?	NO N/A, South Dakota does not have a personal income tax
State Tax Deferred Earnings/ Withdrawals?	NO N/A, South Dakota does not have a personal income tax
Financial Aid Benefits?	NO
State Matching Grants?	NO
Reward Programs?	NO
Direct-sold plan fees:	0.42% - 0.88%
Advisor-sold plan fees:	0.71% - 2.33%
Enrollment Fees:	$0
Investment Option Type(s):	Age-based, Capital Preservation, Equity, Fixed Income ,
Min. Initial Contribution:	Minimum initial contribution: $1,000.00
Minimum Subsequent:	Minimum subsequent contribution: $50.00
Max. Total Contribution:	Maximum total contribution: $350,000.00
Investment Manager(s):	Allianz, Dimensional Fund Advisors, Dodge and Cox, Metropolitan West, Morgan Stanley, PIMCO, The Boston Company Asset Management, TIAA-CREF, Voya Investment Management ,

Tennessee	TNStars College Savings 529 Program	Tennessee Baccalaureate Education System Trust Prepaid Plan
Plan Type(s):	Direct-sold	Prepaid
Plan Website:	http://www.tnstars.com/	http://www.tnbest.com/
Plan Residency:	NO No state residency requirements.	YES Account owner or beneficiary must be state resident.
State Tax Credit or Deduction?	NO	NO
State Tax Deferred Earnings/ Withdrawals?	YES Pursuant to Tennessee Code Annotated 49-7-822 all assets, income and distributions of all college savings plans defined in Section 529 of the Internal Revenue Code are exempt from any state, county or municipal tax.	YES Pursuant to Tennessee Code Annotated 49-7-822 all assets, income and distributions of all college savings plans defined in Section 529 of the Internal Revenue Code are exempt from any state, county or municipal tax.
Financial Aid Benefits?	NO	NO
State Matching Grants?	YES A program of the Tennessee Treasury Department, Tennessee Investments Preparing Scholars, TIPS, is a matching grant program offering incentives to participate in the TNStars® College Savings 529 Program to Tennessee residents meeting certain household income requirements. When a qualifying family establishes a TNStars® account and enrolls a beneficiary in the TIPS program, the state will provide a 4-to-1 matching contribution. That's $100 for every $25 contributed by the account holder. Beneficiaries can receive a maximum match of $500 per year for up to three years.	NO
Reward Programs?	NO	NO
Direct-sold plan fees:	0% - 0.35%	This is a prepaid plan.
Advisor-sold plan fees:	This is a direct-sold plan.	This is a prepaid plan.
Enrollment Fees:	$0	$0
Investment Option Type(s):	Age-based, Blended, Equity, Fixed Income ,	
Min. Initial Contribution:	Minimum initial contribution: $25.00	Minimum initial contribution: $0.00
Minimum Subsequent:	Minimum subsequent contribution: $0.00	Minimum subsequent contribution: $0.00
Max. Total Contribution:	Maximum total contribution: $350,000.00	Maximum total contribution: $350,000.00
Investment Manager(s):	Tennessee Department of Treasury	State Treasury

Data provided by College Savings Plan Network, an affiliate of the National Association of State Treasurers. Visit http://plans.collegesavings.org/planComparison.aspx for more information.

Texas	Texas Tuition Promise Fund	Texas College Savings Plan
Plan Type(s):	Prepaid	Direct-sold
Plan Website:	https://www.texastuitionpromisefund.com/	https://www.texascollegesavings.com/
Plan Residency:	YES Account owner or beneficiary must be state resident.	NO No state residency requirements.
State Tax Credit or Deduction?	NO Texas does not have a state income tax. Earnings are federal tax exempt if the account is used for a qualified educational purpose.	NO
State Tax Deferred Earnings/ Withdrawals?	NO Texas does not have a state income tax on individuals. Earnings are federal tax exempt if the account is used for a qualified educational purpose.	YES Texas does not have a state income tax and unable to provide state tax credits.
Financial Aid Benefits?	YES Texas law provides that assets in a Texas Tuition Promise Fund account may not be considered in determining eligibility for Texas state-funded student financial aid.	YES Under Section 56.007, Texas Education Code, a Texas College Savings Plan account may not be considered an asset or otherwise included as income or other financial resources for the purpose of determining eligibility for a TEXAS grant or any other state-funded student financial assistance.
State Matching Grants?	YES The Texas Match the Promise Foundation offers scholarship awards of matching tuition units to eligible applicants who are beneficiaries of Texas Tuition Promise Fund accounts.	NO
Reward Programs?	NO	NO
Direct-sold plan fees:	This is a prepaid plan.	0.5716% - 0.9772%
Advisor-sold plan fees:	This is a prepaid plan.	This is a direct-sold plan.
Enrollment Fees:	$25	$0
Investment Option Type(s):	Plan allows families to prepay certain higher education expenses, go to plan detail for more information.	Age-based, Blended, Capital Preservation, Equity, Fixed Income
Min. Initial Contribution:	Minimum initial contribution: $0.00	Minimum initial contribution: $25.00
Minimum Subsequent:	Minimum subsequent contribution: $0.00	Minimum subsequent contribution: $15.00
Max. Total Contribution:	Maximum total contribution: $370,000.00	Maximum total contribution: $370,000.00
Investment Manager(s):	Dodge and Cox, Eaton Vance, ETF, Grantham Mayo (GMO), PIMCO, Vanguard, William Blair ,	Artisan, Dimensional Fund Advisors, Dodge and Cox, Dreyfus Corporation, T. Rowe Price, Vanguard

Data provided by College Savings Plans Network, an affiliate of the National Association of State Treasurers.
Visit http://plans.collegesavings.org/planComparison.aspx for more information.

Texas	LoneStar 529 Plan	Texas Guaranteed Tuition Plan
Plan Type(s):	Advisor-sold	Prepaid
Plan Website:	https://www.lonestar529.com/	http://www.tgtp.org/
Plan Residency:	NO No state residency requirements.	YES Account owner or beneficiary must be state resident.
State Tax Credit or Deduction?	NO	NO The state of Texas does not have a state income tax. Earnings are exempt from federal tax if the account is used for a qualified educational purpose.
State Tax Deferred Earnings/ Withdrawals?	YES Tax Incentives Anyone can benefit from the tax advantages of the LoneStar 529 Plan, regardless of income level, tax bracket or financial situation. Tax-free Growth Because earnings in 529 plans are not subject to federal or state taxes, the wind is at your back as assets in the account grow. Tax-free Withdrawal You can withdraw funds in a 529 plan account to pay for Qualified Higher Education Expenses without incurring federal taxes, if the money is used for other purposes, the earnings portion of the withdrawal is subject to ordinary federal income tax, and any applicable state income tax and an additional 10% federal tax.	NO The state of Texas does not have a state income tax. Earnings are exempt from federal tax if the account is used for a qualified educational purpose.
Financial Aid Benefits?	YES Under Section 56.007, Texas Education Code, a LoneStar 529 Plan account may not be considered an asset or otherwise included as income or other financial resources for the purpose of determining eligibility for a TEXAS grant or any other state-funded student financial assistance.	YES Texas 529 plan accounts may not be considered an asset or otherwise included as income or other financial resources for the purpose of determining eligibility for a TEXAS grant or any other state-funded student financial assistance.
State Matching Grants?	NO	NO The state's matching program only applies to the Texas Tuition Promise Fund.
Reward Programs?	NO	NO
Direct-sold plan fees:	This is an advisor-sold plan.	This is a prepaid plan.
Advisor-sold plan fees:	0.7853% - 2.5053%	This is a prepaid plan.
Enrollment Fees:	$0	$0
Investment Option Type(s):	Age-based, Blended, Capital Preservation, Equity, Fixed Income	Plan allows families to prepay certain higher education expenses, go to plan detail for more information.
Min. Initial Contribution:	Minimum initial contribution: $25.00	Minimum initial contribution: $0.00
Minimum Subsequent:	Minimum subsequent contribution: $15.00	Minimum subsequent contribution: $0.00
Max. Total Contribution:	Maximum total contribution: $370,000.00	Maximum total contribution: $0.00
Investment Manager(s):	Artisan, DFA, Dodge and Cox, Dreyfus Corporation, T. Rowe Price, Templeton, TIAA-CREF, William Blair	Advantus, Grantham Mayo (GMO), Northern Trust Investments, N.A., Northern Trust TIPS Index, Rhumbline Advisors, Shenkman

Data provided by College Savings Plan Network, an affiliate of the National Association of State Treasurers. Visit http://plans.collegesavings.org/planComparison.aspx for more information.

Utah

my529

Plan Type(s):	Direct-sold
Plan Website:	http://www.my529.org/
Plan Residency:	NO No state residency requirements.
State Tax Credit or Deduction?	YES Utah taxpayers, including Utah trusts, who are account owners may file for a Utah tax credit. Utah Corporations may file for a Utah tax deduction. The 2020 individual Utah state tax credit amount is contributions up to $2,040 ($4,080 filing jointly) per beneficiary multiplied by 5.00%, equaling $102 ($204 filing jointly) per beneficiary. For Utah Trusts, the 2020 Utah state tax credit amount is contributions up to $2,040 per beneficiary multiplied by 5.00%, equaling $102 per beneficiary. For Corporations, the 2020 Utah state tax deduction amount is contributions up to $2,040 per beneficiary. A joint tax benefit is not allowed for my529 institutional accounts such as trusts or corporations.
State Tax Deferred Earnings/ Withdrawals?	YES The earnings on any disbursement used for qualified higher education expenses are currently exempt from federal taxes and Utah state income tax.
Financial Aid Benefits?	YES Olene S. Walker Transition to Adult Living (TAL) Scholarship The TAL Scholarship was designed to assist qualified youth who are transitioning from the Utah foster care system to complete a post-secondary education program at one of the Utah System of Higher Education (USHE) institutions. my529 funds scholarships as part of the newly initiated Transition to Adult Living (TAL) program.
State Matching Grants?	NO
Reward Programs?	NO
Direct-sold plan fees:	0% - 0.177%
Advisor-sold plan fees:	This is a direct-sold plan.
Enrollment Fees:	$0
Investment Option Type(s):	Age-based, Blended, Capital Preservation, Equity, Fixed Income
Min. Initial Contribution:	Minimum initial contribution: $0.00
Minimum Subsequent:	Minimum subsequent contribution: $0.00
Max. Total Contribution:	Maximum total contribution: $500,000.00
Investment Manager(s):	Dimensional Fund Advisors, Office of the Utah State Treasurer, PIMCO, Sallie Mae Bank, Sallie Mae Bank and U.S. Bank, The Vanguard Group®, US Bank

Vermont

Vermont Higher Education Investment Plan

Plan Type(s):	Direct-sold
Plan Website:	https://www.vheip.org/
Plan Residency:	Unknown At this time, residency information has not been added for this plan.
State Tax Credit or Deduction?	YES A State taxpayer (or, in the case of a married couple filing jointly, each spouse) is eligible for a nonrefundable tax credit of 10% of the first $2,500 per Beneficiary contributed to an Account in the Plan in each taxable year beginning on and after January 1, 2007 (i.e., a nonrefundable tax credit of up to $250 per Beneficiary per year).
State Tax Deferred Earnings/ Withdrawals?	YES The earnings on your Account are deferred for State income tax purposes until withdrawal. As long as withdrawals from your Account are used for the Beneficiary's Qualified Higher Education Expenses, the earnings portion of the withdrawals will not be subject to State of Vermont income taxation.
Financial Aid Benefits?	NO
State Matching Grants?	NO
Reward Programs?	NO
Direct-sold plan fees:	0.39% - 39%
Advisor-sold plan fees:	This is a direct-sold plan.
Enrollment Fees:	$0
Investment Option Type(s):	Age-based, Blended, Equity, Fixed Income, Guaranteed
Min. Initial Contribution:	Minimum initial contribution: $15.00
Minimum Subsequent:	Minimum subsequent contribution: $15.00
Max. Total Contribution:	Maximum total contribution: $352,800.00
Investment Manager(s):	CLS Investments, LLC, TIAA-CREF

Data provided by College Savings Plans Network, an affiliate of the National Association of State Treasurers. Visit http://plans.collegesavings.org/planComparison.aspx for more information.

Virginia

CollegeAmerica

Plan Type(s):	**Advisor-sold**
Plan Website:	https://www.americanfunds.com/college.html
Plan Residency:	**NO** No state residency requirements.
State Tax Credit or Deduction?	**YES** CollegeAmerica Account Owners who file a Virginia state individual income tax return can deduct CollegeAmerica contributions from their Virginia taxable income. The deduction is limited to $4,000 per calendar year per VA529 account, or the amount contributed to each VA529 account during the year, whichever is less, with unlimited carry forward until the full amount of the contributions have been deducted. The $4,000 per calendar year limit does not apply to account owners who are age 70 or above, who may deduct the entire amount of their contributions in a single tax year. If an account is cancelled for a reason other than the student's death, disability, receipt of a scholarship, or Rollover to another VA529 account, any amount of the refund previously deducted from the account owner's Virginia taxable income as a result of contributions to the cancelled CollegeAmerica Account must be added back to the Account Owner's Virginia taxable income in the year the refund is received, in addition to any federal tax consequences.
State Tax Deferred Earnings/ Withdrawals?	**YES** Any earnings on CollegeAmerica accounts grow tax free at both the federal and state level, which means that the account owner does not have to pay federal or state tax on any interest or the increased account value each year. If the account is used for qualified higher education expenses, the earnings are tax free. All nonqualified distributions (those not used for qualified higher education expenses) are subject to federal and state income tax on the earnings portion of the distribution. The earnings portion of any amount refunded in one of these cases is subject to federal income tax in the tax year in which the refund is received, but is exempt from Virginia state income tax. The Virginia state income tax exemption is still applicable to distributions made due to the Beneficiary's death, disability or receipt of a scholarship.
Financial Aid Benefits?	**YES** Ownership of a CollegeAmerica account will not be taken into account when determining a student's eligibility for Virginia financial aid. CollegeAmerica Benefits do not affect a student's eligibility for a Virginia Tuition Assistance Grant for Virginia residents who attend an eligible, independent, nonprofit institution of higher education in Virginia.
State Matching Grants?	**NO**
Reward Programs?	**NO**
Direct-sold plan fees:	This is an advisor-sold plan.
Advisor-sold plan fees:	0.5% - 2.21%
Enrollment Fees:	$0
Investment Option Type(s):	Age-based, Blended, Capital Preservation, Equity, Fixed Income
Min. Initial Contribution:	Minimum initial contribution: $250.00
Minimum Subsequent:	Minimum subsequent contribution: $50.00
Max. Total Contribution:	Maximum total contribution: $500,000.00
Investment Manager(s):	Capital Research and Management Company, Capital Research and Management Company, Capital Research and Management Company, Capital Research and Management Company, Capital Research and Management Company

Data provided by College Savings Plan Network, an affiliate of the National Association of State Treasurers. Visit http://plans.collegesavings.org/planComparison.aspx for more information.

Virginia | Prepaid529

Plan Type(s):	**Prepaid**
Plan Website:	https://www.virginia529.com/current-savers/prepaid/
Plan Residency:	**YES** Account owner or beneficiary must be state resident.
State Tax Credit or Deduction?	**YES** Prepaid529 Account Owners who file a Virginia state individual income tax return can deduct Prepaid529 Payments from their Virginia taxable income. The deduction is limited to $4,000 per calendar year per VA529 account, or the amount contributed to each VA529 account during the year, whichever is less, with unlimited carry forward until the full amount of the Payments has been deducted. The $4,000 per calendar year limit does not apply to account owners who are age 70 or above, who may deduct the entire amount of their payments in a single tax year. If an account is cancelled for a reason other than the student's death, disability, receipt of a scholarship, or Rollover to another VA529 account, any amount of the refund previously deducted from the account owner's Virginia taxable income as a result of payments to the cancelled Prepaid529 Account must be added back to the Account Owner's Virginia taxable income in the year the refund is received, in addition to any federal tax consequences.
State Tax Deferred Earnings/ Withdrawals?	**YES** Any earnings on Prepaid529 contracts grow tax free at both the federal and state level, which means that the account owner does not have to pay federal or state tax on any interest or the increased contract value each year. If the contract is used for qualified higher education expenses, the earnings are tax free. All nonqualified distributions (those not used for qualified higher education expenses) are subject to federal and state income tax on the earnings portion of the distribution. The earnings portion of any amount refunded in one of these cases is subject to federal income tax in the tax year in which the refund is received, but is exempt from Virginia state income tax. The Virginia state income tax exemption is still applicable to distributions made due to the Beneficiary's death, disability or receipt of a scholarship.
Financial Aid Benefits?	**YES** Ownership of a Prepaid529 Contract will not be taken into account when determining a student's eligibility for Virginia financial aid. Prepaid529 Benefits do not affect a student's eligibility for a Virginia Tuition Assistance Grant for Virginia residents who attend an eligible, independent, nonprofit institution of higher education in Virginia.
State Matching Grants?	**NO**
Reward Programs?	**NO**
Direct-sold plan fees:	This is a prepaid plan.
Advisor-sold plan fees:	This is a prepaid plan.
Enrollment Fees:	$0
Investment Option Type(s):	Not applicable, go to plan detail for more information.
Min. Initial Contribution:	Minimum initial contribution: $0.00
Minimum Subsequent:	Minimum subsequent contribution: $0.00
Max. Total Contribution:	Maximum total contribution: $500,000.00
Investment Manager(s):	Aberdeen, Adams Street Partners, LLC, Advent Capital, Aether Investment Partners, American Funds, Aventura Holdings, LLC, BlackRock, Blackstone Partners, Commonfund Capital Inc., CS Transition, DFA, Dreyfus Corporation, Ferox Capital, Golub Capital, Horsley Bridge Partners, LGT Capital Partners, Neuberger Berman LLC, Other - Acadian Non-US, Other - UBS Trumbull, PGIM Fixed Income, Private Advisors LLC, Sands Capital Management, Inc., Schroders Investment Management, Shenkman, State Treasury, Stone Harbor Investment Partners, The Vanguard Group®, Thompson, Siegel & Walmsley, Inc., Wellington Capital Management, Westfield Capital Management

Virginia

Invest529

Plan Type(s):	Direct-sold
Plan Website:	http://www.virginia529.com/
Plan Residency:	NO No state residency requirements.
State Tax Credit or Deduction?	YES Invest529 Account Owners who file a Virginia state individual income tax return can deduct Invest529 Payments from their Virginia taxable income. The deduction is limited to $4,000 per calendar year per VA529 account, or the amount contributed to each VA529 account during the year, whichever is less, with unlimited carry forward until the full amount of the Payments has been deducted. The $4,000 per calendar year limit does not apply to account owners who are age 70 or above, who may deduct the entire amount of their payments in a single tax year. If an account is cancelled for a reason other than the student's death, disability, receipt of a scholarship, or Rollover to another VA529 account, any amount of the refund previously deducted from the account owner's Virginia taxable income as a result of payments to the cancelled Invest529 Account must be added back to the Account Owner's Virginia taxable income in the year the refund is received, in addition to any federal tax consequences.
State Tax Deferred Earnings/ Withdrawals?	YES Any earnings on Invest529 accounts grow tax free at both the federal and state level, which means that the account owner does not have to pay federal or state tax on any interest or the increased account value each year. If the account is used for qualified higher education expenses, the earnings are tax free. All non-qualified distributions (those not used for qualified higher education expenses) are subject to federal and state income tax on the earnings portion of the distribution. The earnings portion of any amount refunded in one of these cases is subject to federal income tax in the tax year in which the refund is received, but is exempt from Virginia state income tax. The Virginia state income tax exemption Is still applicable to distributions made due to the Beneficiary's death, disability or receipt of a scholarship.
Financial Aid Benefits?	YES Ownership of a Invest529 account will not be taken into account when determining a student's eligibility for Virginia financial aid. Invest529 Benefits do not affect a student's eligibility for a Virginia Tuition Assistance Grant for Virginia residents who attend an eligible, independent, nonprofit institution of higher education in Virginia.
State Matching Grants?	NO
Reward Programs?	NO
Direct-sold plan fees:	0.09% - 0.62%
Advisor-sold plan fees:	This is a direct-sold plan.
Enrollment Fees:	$0 - $50
Investment Option Type(s):	Age-based, Blended, Equity, Fixed Income ,
Min. Initial Contribution:	Minimum initial contribution: $0.00
Minimum Subsequent:	Minimum subsequent contribution: $0.00
Max. Total Contribution:	Maximum total contribution: None
Investment Manager(s):	Aberdeen, American Funds, Blackstone, DFA, INVESCO Institutional (N.A.), Inc., Multiple Investment Managers, Other - Atlantic Union Bank, Other - UBS Trumbull, Parnassus Investments, PGIM, Rothschild Asset Management, Inc., Sands Capital Management, Inc., Stone Harbor Investment Partners, Templeton, The Vanguard Group®, Wellington Capital Management

Washington	Guaranteed Education Tuition (GET)	DreamAhead College Investment Plan
Plan Type(s):	Prepaid	Direct-sold
Plan Website:	http://www.get.wa.gov/	https://dreamahead.wa.gov/
Plan Residency:	YES Account owner or beneficiary must be state resident.	NO No state residency requirements.
State Tax Credit or Deduction?	NO Washington state does not have a state income tax.	NO Washington state does not have a state income tax.
State Tax Deferred Earnings/ Withdrawals?	NO Washington state does not have a state income tax.	NO Washington state does not have a state income tax.
Financial Aid Benefits?	YES •State financial aid programs: Washington state does not consider the value of GET accounts in determining a family's eligibility for state financial aid. The state considers current family income only. •Federal financial aid programs: If the parent is the account owner, the GET account is considered an asset of the parent and treated like any other parental asset in determining a family's eligibility for federal financial aid.	YES •State financial aid programs: Washington state does not consider the value of DreamAhead accounts in determining a family's eligibility for state financial aid. The state considers current family income only. •Federal financial aid programs: If the parent is the account owner, the DreamAhead account is considered an asset of the parent and treated like any other parental asset in determining a family's eligibility for federal financial aid.
State Matching Grants?	NO No matching grant program is currently in place.	NO No matching grant program is currently in place.
Reward Programs?	NO	NO
Direct-sold plan fees:	This is a prepaid plan.	0.259% - 0.4%
Advisor-sold plan fees:	This is a prepaid plan.	This is a direct-sold plan.
Enrollment Fees:	$50	$0
Investment Option Type(s):	Plan allows families to prepay certain higher education expenses, go to plan detail for more information.	Age-based, Blended, Capital Preservation, Equity, Fixed Income
Min. Initial Contribution:	Minimum initial contribution: $0.00	Minimum initial contribution: $25.00
Minimum Subsequent:	Minimum subsequent contribution: $0.00	Minimum subsequent contribution: $5.00
Max. Total Contribution:	Maximum total contribution: $0.00	Maximum total contribution: $500,000.00
Investment Manager(s):	Washington State Investment Board (WSIB)	Lockwood Advisors, Inc.

Data provided by College Savings Plans Network, an affiliate of the National Association of State Treasurers. Visit http://plans.collegesavings.org/planComparison.aspx for more information.

West Virginia	SMART529 WV Direct	The Hartford SMART529	SMART529 Select
Plan Type(s):	Direct-sold	Advisor-sold	Direct-sold
Plan Website:	http://www.smart529.com/	http://www.hartfordfunds.com/college-saving/overview-smart-529.individual-investors.html	http://www.smart529select.com/
Plan Residency:	YES Account owner or beneficiary must be state resident.	NO No state residency requirements.	NO No state residency requirements.
State Tax Credit or Deduction?	YES WV taxpayer may deduct all contributions to their SMART529 accounts from the federal adjusted gross income on their WV Personal Income Tax Return. They are allowed the deduction for contributions for each Designated Beneficiary and may carry the amount forward for up to five years. The WV state deduction is subject to recapture for non-qualified distributions.	YES WV taxpayer may deduct all contributions to their SMART529 accounts from the federal adjusted gross income on their WV Personal Income Tax Return. They are allowed the deduction for contributions for each Designated Beneficiary and may carry the amount forward for up to five years. The WV state deduction is subject to recapture for non-qualified distributions.	YES WV taxpayer may deduct all contributions to their SMART529 accounts from the federal adjusted gross income on their WV Personal Income Tax Return. They are allowed the deduction for contributions for each Designated Beneficiary and may carry the amount forward for up to five years. The WV state deduction is subject to recapture for non-qualified distributions.
State Tax Deferred Earnings/ Withdrawals?	YES Earnings can accumulate tax-deferred; withdrawals for qualified higher education expenses are free from federal and WV income taxes.	YES Earnings can accumulate tax-deferred; withdrawals for qualified higher education expenses are free from federal and WV income taxes.	YES Earnings can accumulate tax-deferred; withdrawals for qualified higher education expenses are free from federal and WV income taxes.
Financial Aid Benefits?	NO	NO	NO
State Matching Grants?	NO SMART529 offers WV residents a $100 grant for babies under one year of age or adopted children who have not reached the first anniversary of their adoption date. See eligibility rules.	NO SMART529 offers WV residents a $100 grant for babies under one year of age or adopted children who have not reached the first anniversary of their adoption date. See eligibility rules.	NO SMART529 offers WV residents a $100 grant for babies under one year of age or adopted children who have not reached the first anniversary of their adoption date. See eligibility rules.
Reward Programs?	YES SMART529 has partnered with Upromise.	YES SMART529 has partnered with Upromise.	YES SMART529 has partnered with Upromise.
Direct-sold plan fees:	0.12% - 0.22%	This is an advisor-sold plan.	0.57% - 0.67%
Advisor-sold plan fees:	This is a direct-sold plan.	0.54% - 2.08%	This is a direct-sold plan.
Enrollment Fees:	$0	$0	$0
Investment Option Type(s):	Age-based, Blended, Equity, Fixed Income ,	Age-based, Blended, Capital Preservation, Equity, Fixed Income	Age-based, Blended, Fixed Income
Min. Initial Contribution:	Minimum initial contribution: $0.00	Minimum initial contribution: $250.00	Minimum initial contribution: $250.00
Minimum Subsequent:	Minimum subsequent contribution: $0.00	Minimum subsequent contribution: $25.00	Minimum subsequent contribution: $25.00
Max. Total Contribution:	Maximum total contribution: $400,000.00	Maximum total contribution: $400,000.00	Maximum total contribution: $400,000.00
Investment Manager(s):	INVESCO Institutional (N.A.), Inc., The Vanguard Group®	BlackRock iShares, INVESCO Institutional (N.A.), Inc., MFS Investment Management, The Hartford Mutual Funds	Dimensional Fund Advisors

Data provided by College Savings Plan Network, an affiliate of the National Association of State Treasurers. Visit http://plans.collegesavings.org/planComparison.aspx for more information.

Wisconsin	Edvest College Savings Plan	Tomorrow's Scholar College Savings Plan
Plan Type(s):	Direct-sold	Advisor-sold
Plan Website:	http://www.edvest.com/	http://www.tomorrowsscholar.com/
Plan Residency:	NO No state residency requirements.	NO No state residency requirements.
State Tax Credit or Deduction?	YES For tax year 2019, contributions up to $3,280 per contributor per beneficiary reduce Wisconsin taxable income. This amount may be increased each year with inflation. Contributions in excess may be carried forward for one or more years for additional subtractions to state income. Contributors do not need to be the account owner to claim the benefit. Deadline is April 15 of the year following the reported tax year. The maximum account limit is $505,000 as of November 20, 2019.	YES For tax year 2019, contributions up to $3,340 per contributor per beneficiary reduce Wisconsin taxable income. This amount may be increased each year with inflation. Contributions in excess may be carried forward for one or more years for additional subtractions to state income. Contributors do not need to be the account owner to claim the benefit. Deadline is April 15 of the year following the reported tax year. The maximum account limit is $505,000 per beneficiary as of November 20, 2019.
State Tax Deferred Earnings/ Withdrawals?	YES Program earnings are exempt from Wisconsin state income tax if the savings are used for qualified higher education expenses.	YES Program earnings are exempt from Wisconsin state income tax if the savings are used for qualified higher education expenses.
Financial Aid Benefits?	YES Wisconsin law specifies that Program assets will NOT affect a beneficiary's eligibility for State-funded financial aid.	YES Wisconsin law specifies that Program assets will NOT affect a beneficiary's eligibility for State-funded financial aid.
State Matching Grants?	NO	NO
Reward Programs?	NO	NO
Direct-sold plan fees:	0% - 0.38%	This is an advisor-sold plan.
Advisor-sold plan fees:	This is a direct-sold plan.	0.23% - 2.3%
Enrollment Fees:	$0	$0
Investment Option Type(s):	Age-based, Blended, Capital Preservation, Equity, Fixed Income, Guaranteed,	Age-based, Blended, Equity, Fixed Income, Guaranteed
Min. Initial Contribution:	Minimum initial contribution: $25.00	Minimum initial contribution: $250.00
Minimum Subsequent:	Minimum subsequent contribution: $25.00	Minimum subsequent contribution: $25.00
Max. Total Contribution:	Maximum total contribution: $472,000.00	Maximum total contribution: $472,000.00
Investment Manager(s):	Dimensional Fund Advisors, Franklin Templeton Investments, Metropolitan West, Multiple Managers, T. Rowe Price, TIAA-CREF	Baillie Gifford, BlackRock, Brandywine Global Asset Management, Columbia Management Investment Advisers, LLC and its affiliates, Credit Suisse, Delaware Investments, Hahn Capital Management, Lazard Asset Management, LSV Asset Management, Multiple Managers, Northern Trust Investments, N.A., Other - Brookfield, Other - Brookfield, Polaris, TIAA-CREF, Van Eck Associates, Voya Investment Management, Wellington Management

All States

Private College 529 Plan

Plan Type(s):	**Prepaid**
Plan Website:	https://www.privatecollege529.com/OFI529/home.jsp
Plan Residency:	**NO** No state residency requirements.
State Tax Credit or Deduction?	**Unknown**
State Tax Deferred Earnings/ Withdrawals?	**Unknown**
Financial Aid Benefits?	**Unknown**
State Matching Grants?	**Unknown**
Reward Programs?	**Unknown**
Direct-sold plan fees:	This is a prepaid plan.
Advisor-sold plan fees:	This is a prepaid plan.
Enrollment Fees:	$0
Investment Option Type(s):	
Min. Initial Contribution:	Minimum initial contribution: $0.00
Minimum Subsequent:	Minimum subsequent contribution: $0.00
Max. Total Contribution:	Maximum total contribution: $0.00
Investment Manager(s):	OppenheimerFunds Inc.

Glossary

529 Plan:

The number refers to the section of the United States Internal Revenue Code that deals with qualified tuition programs. 529 plans are education savings plans enabled by the provisions of section 529.

Coverdell Education Savings Accounts:

These education savings plans are tax-advantaged like 529 plans; however, the annual cap on contributions to a Coverdell ESA is currently set at $2,000 per year.

Frontloading:

To put a large amount into an investment plan early on in order to benefit maximally from growth over time.

Prepaid Tuition Plan:

Allows you to purchase credit hours at today's tuition rates that can be used by your child in the future.

Tax-advantaged:

Describes an investment, account, or plan that is exempt from taxation, tax-deferred, or that offers some other type of tax benefit.

Trust:

A legal and fiduciary arrangement allowing a third party, or a trustee, to hold assets on behalf of a beneficiary or beneficiaries. Trusts allow you to define your own terms about disbursements and other matters.

UGMA / UTMA. Uniform Gifts to Minors Act (UGMA) and Uniform Transfers to Minors Act (UTMA):

These acts allow minors to own assets. Individuals can establish UGMA accounts on behalf of minors as beneficiaries and this eliminates the need for attorneys to set up trust funds.

https://greyhouse.weissratings.com

Financial Ratings Series, published by Weiss Ratings and Grey House Publishing offers libraries, schools, universities and the business community a wide range of investing, banking, insurance and financial literacy tools. Visit www.greyhouse.com or https://greyhouse.weissratings.com for more information about the titles and online tools below.

- Weiss Ratings Consumer Guides
- Weiss Ratings Financial Literacy Basics
- Weiss Ratings Financial Literacy: Planning for the Future
- Weiss Ratings Financial Literacy: How to Become an Investor
- Weiss Ratings Guide to Banks
- Weiss Ratings Guide to Credit Unions
- Weiss Ratings Guide to Health Insurers
- Weiss Ratings Guide to Life & Annuity Insurers
- Weiss Ratings Guide to Property & Casualty Insurers
- Weiss Ratings Investment Research Guide to Bond & Money Market Mutual Funds
- Weiss Ratings Investment Research Guide to Exchange-Traded Funds
- Weiss Ratings Investment Research Guide to Stock Mutual Funds
- Weiss Ratings Investment Research Guide to Stocks
- Weiss Ratings Medicare Supplement Insurance Buyers Guide
- Financial Ratings Series Online – **https://greyhouse.weissratings.com**